POEMS OF SIDNEY LANIER

POEMS OF
Sidney Lanier

EDITED BY
MARY DAY LANIER

AFTERWORD
FOR THIS EDITION BY
JOHN HOLLANDER

THE UNIVERSITY OF GEORGIA PRESS
ATHENS

Afterword by John Hollander copyright © 1981, by the
University of Georgia Press, Athens, Georgia 30602

Printed in the United States of America

96 95 94 93 92   C   7 6 5 4 3

Library of Congress Cataloging in Publication Data
Lanier, Sidney, 1842-1881.
    Poems of Sidney Lanier.
    Reprint of the 1916 ed. published by Scribner, New
York.
    Includes bibliographical references.
    I. Lanier, Mary Day.
PS2205.A2L35   1981   811'.4   80-29576
                 ISBN 0-8203-0560-X

Poems of Sidney Lanier, edited by Lanier's wife, Mary,
was first published in 1884 by Charles Scribner's Sons,
New York. This edition has been reproduced from the
1916 edition of that work.

CONTENTS.

CONTENTS.

CONTENTS.

MEMORIAL.

BECAUSE I believe that Sidney Lanier was much
more than a clever artisan in rhyme and metre ; be-
cause he will, I think, take his final rank with the
first princes of American song, I am glad to provide
this slight memorial. There is sufficient material in
his letters for an extremely interesting biography,
which could be properly prepared only by his wife.
These pages can give but a sketch of his life and
work.

Sidney Lanier was born at Macon, Ga., on the
third of February, 1842. His earliest known ances-
tor of the name was Jerome Lanier, a Huguenot
refugee, who was attached to the court of Queen
Elizabeth, very likely as a musical composer ; and
whose son, Nicholas, was in high favor with James I.
and Charles I., as director of music, painter, and
political envoy ; and whose grandson, Nicholas, held a
similar position in the court of Charles II. A portrait
of the elder Nicholas Lanier, by his friend Van Dyck,
was sold, with other pictures belonging to Charles
I., after his execution. The younger Nicholas was
the first Marshal, or presiding officer, of the Soci-
ety of Musicians, incorporated at the Restoration,
" for the improvement of the science and the interest

of its professors;" and it is remarkable that four others of the name of Lanier were among the few incorporators, one of them, John Lanier, very likely father of the Sir John Lanier who fought as Major-General at the Battle of the Boyne, and fell gloriously at Steinkirk along with the brave Douglas.

The American branch of the family originated as early as 1716 with the immigration of Thomas Lanier, who settled with other colonists on a grant of land ten miles square, which includes the present city of Richmond, Va. One of the family, a Thomas Lanier, married an aunt of George Washington. The family is somewhat widely scattered, chiefly in the Southern States.

The father of our poet was Robert S. Lanier, a lawyer still living in Macon, Ga. His mother was Mary Anderson, a Virginian of Scotch descent, from a family that supplied members of the House of Burgesses of Virginia for many years and in more than one generation, and was gifted in poetry, music, and oratory.

His earliest passion was for music. As a child he learned to play, almost without instruction, on every kind of instrument he could find; and while yet a boy he played the flute, organ, piano, violin, guitar, and banjo, especially devoting himself to the flute in deference to his father, who feared for him the powerful fascination of the violin. For it was the violin-voice that, above all others, commanded his soul. He has related that during his college days it would sometimes so exalt him in rapture, that presently he would sink from his solitary music-worship into a deep trance, thence to awake, alone, on the floor of his room, sorely shaken in nerve.

In after years more than one listener remarked the strange violin effects which he conquered from the flute. His devotion to music rather alarmed than pleased his friends, and while it was here that he first discovered that he possessed decided genius, he for some time shared the early notion of his parents, that it was an unworthy pursuit, and he rather repressed his taste. He did not then know by what inheritance it had come to him, nor how worthy is the art.

At the age of fourteen he entered the sophomore class of Oglethorpe College, an institution under Presbyterian control near Midway, Ga., which had not vitality enough to survive the war. He graduated in 1860, at the age of eighteen, with the first honors of his class, having lost a year during which he took a clerkship in the Macon post-office. At least one genuine impulse was received in this college life, and that proceeded from Professor James Woodrow, who was then one of Sidney's teachers, and who has since been connected with the University and Theological Seminary in Columbia, S. C. During the last weeks of his life Mr. Lanier stated that he owed to Professor Woodrow the strongest and most valuable stimulus of his youth. Immediately on his graduation he was called to a tutorship in the college, which position he held until the outbreak of the war.

And here, with some hesitation, I record, as a true biography requires, the development of his consciousness of possessing real genius. One with this gift has a right to know it, just as others know if they possess talent or shiftiness of resource. While we do not talk so much of genius now as we did a generation ago, we can yet recognize the differ-

ence between the fervor of that divine birth and the
cantering of the livery Pegasus forth and back,
along the vulgar boulevards over which facile talent
rides his daily hack.   Only once or twice, in his own
private note-book, or in a letter to his wife when it
was needful, in sickness and loneliness, to strengthen
her will and his by testifying his own deepest con-
sciousness of power, did he whisper the assurance of
his strength.   But he knew it, and she knew it, and
it gave his will a peace in toil, a sun-lit peace, not-
withstanding sickness, or want, or misapprehension,
calm above the zone of clouds.

As I have said, his genius he first fully discovered in
music.   I copy from his pencilled college note-book
what cannot have been written after he was eighteen
years old.   The boy had been discussing the question
with himself how far his inclinations were to be re-
garded as indicating his best capacities and his duties.
He says :

" The point which I wish to settle is merely, by
what method shall I ascertain what I am fit for, as
preliminary to ascertaining God's will with reference
to me ; or ascertaining what my inclinations are, as
preliminary to ascertaining what my capacities are,
that is, what I am fit for.   I am more than all per-
plexed by this fact, that the prime inclination, that
is, natural bent (which I have checked, though) of
my nature is to music ; and for that I have the great-
est talent ; indeed, not boasting, for God gave it me,
I have an extraordinary musical talent, and feel it
within me plainly that I could rise as high as any com-
poser.   But I cannot bring myself to believe that I
was intended for a musician, because it seems so small
a business in comparison with other things which, it
seems to me, I might do.   Question here, What is
the province of music in the economy of the world ? "

Similar aspirations he felt at this early age, prob-
ably eighteen, for grand literary labor, as the same
note-book would bear witness. We see here the
boy talking to himself, a boy who had found in him-
self a standard above anything in his fellows.

The breaking out of the war summoned Sidney
Lanier from books to arms. In April, 1861, he en-
listed in the Confederate Army, with the Macon Vol-
unteers of the Second Georgia Battalion, the first
military organization which left Georgia for Vir-
ginia. From his childhood he had had a military
taste. Even as a small boy he had raised a company
of boys armed with bows and arrows, and so well did
he drill them that an honored place was granted
them in the military parades of their elders. Having
volunteered as a private at the age of nineteen, he re-
mained a private till the last year of the war. Three
times he was offered promotion and refused it because
it would separate him from his younger brother, who
was his companion in arms, as their singularly ten-
der devotion would not allow them to be parted. The
first year of service in Virginia was easy and pleasant,
and he spent his abundant leisure in music and the
study of German, French, and Spanish. He was in
the battles of Seven Pines, Drewry's Bluffs, and the
seven days' fighting about Richmond, culminating in
the terrible struggle of Malvern Hill. After this
campaign he was transferred, with his brother, to the
signal service, the joke among his less fortunate com-
panions being that he was selected because he could
play the flute. His headquarters were now for a
short period at Petersburg, where he had the advan-
tage of a small local library, but where he began to
feel the premonitions of that fatal disease, consump-

tion, against which he battled for fifteen years. The regular full inspirations required by the flute probably prolonged his life. In 1863 his detachment was mounted and did service in Virginia and North Carolina. At last the two brothers were separated, it coming in the duty of each to take charge of a vessel which was to run the blockade. Sidney's vessel was captured, and he was for five months in Point Lookout prison, until he was exchanged (with his flute, for he never lost it), near the close of the war. Those were very hard days for him, and a picture of them is given in his "Tiger Lilies," the novel which he wrote two years afterward. It is a luxuriant, unpruned work, written in haste for the press within the space of three weeks, but one which gave rich promise of the poet. A chapter in the middle of the book, introducing the scenes of those four years of struggle, is wholly devoted to a remarkable metaphor, which becomes an allegory and a sermon, in which war is pictured as "a strange, enormous, terrible flower," which "the early spring of 1861 brought to bloom besides innumerable violets and jessamines." He tells how the plant is grown ; what arguments the horticulturists give for cultivating it ; how Christ inveighed against it, and how its shades are damp and its odors unhealthy ; and what a fine specimen was grown the other day in North America by "two wealthy landed proprietors, who combined all their resources of money, of blood, of bones, of tears, of sulphur, and what not, to make this the grandest specimen of modern horticulture." "It is supposed by some," says he, "that seed of this American specimen (now dead) yet remains in the land ; but as for this author (who, with many friends, suffered from the unhealthy odors of the plant), he could find it in his heart to wish fervently that this seed, if there be verily any, might perish in the germ, utterly out of sight and life and memory, and out of the remote hope of resurrection, forever and ever, no matter in whose granary they are cherished!" Through those four years, though earnestly devoted to the cause, and fulfilling his duties with zeal, his horror of war grew to the end. He had entered it in a "crack" regiment, with a dandy uniform, and was first encamped near Norfolk, where the gardens, with the Northern market hopelessly cut off, were given freely to the soldiers, who lived in every luxury; and every man had his sweetheart in Norfolk. But the tyranny and Christlessness of war oppressed him, though he loved the free life in the saddle and under the stars.

In February, 1865, he was released from Point Lookout and undertook the weary return on foot to his home in Georgia, with the twenty-dollar gold piece which he had in his pocket when captured, and which was returned to him, with his other little effects, when he was released. Of course he had the flute, which he had hidden in his sleeve when he entered the prison, and which had earned him some comforts. He reached home March 15th, with his strength utterly exhausted. There followed six weeks of desperate illness, and just as he began to recover from it his beloved mother died of consumption. He himself arose from his sick-bed with pronounced congestion of one lung, but found relief in two months of out-of-door life with an uncle at Point Clear, Mobile Bay. From December, 1865, to April, 1867, he filled a clerkship in Montgomery, Ala., and in the next month made his first visit to New

York on the business of publishing his "Tiger Lilies," written in April. In September, 1867, he took charge of a country academy of nearly a hundred pupils in Prattville, Ala., and was married in December of the same year to Miss Mary Day, daughter of Charles Day, of Macon.

To the years before Mr. Lanier's marriage belong a dozen poems included in this volume. Two of them are translations from the German made during the war; the others are songs and miscellaneous poems, full of flush and force, but not yet moulded by those laws of art of whose authority he had hardly become conscious. His access to books was limited, and he expressed himself more with music than with literature, taking down the notes of birds, and writing music to his own songs or those of Tennyson.

In January, 1868, the next month after his marriage, he suffered his first hemorrhage from the lungs, and returned in May to Macon, in very low health. Here he remained, studying and afterward practising law with his father, until December, 1872. During this period there came, in the spring and summer of 1870, a more alarming decline with settled cough. He went for treatment to New York, where he remained two months, returning in October greatly improved and strong in hope; but again at home he lost ground steadily. He was now fairly engaged in the brave struggle against consumption, which could have but one end. So precarious already was his health that a change of residence was determined on, and in December, 1872, he went to San Antonio, Texas, in search of a permanent home there, leaving his wife and children meanwhile at Macon. But the climate did not prove favorable and he returned in April, 1873.

During these five years a sense of holy obligation, based on the conviction that special talents had been given him, and that the time might be short, rested upon Lanier, until it was impossible to resist it longer. He felt himself called to something other than a country attorney's practice. It was the compulsion of waiting utterance, not yet enfranchised. From Texas he wrote to his wife :

"Were it not for some circumstances which make such a proposition seem absurd in the highest degree, I would think that I am shortly to die, and that my spirit hath been singing its swan-song before dissolution. All day my soul hath been cutting swiftly into the great space of the subtle, unspeakable deep, driven by wind after wind of heavenly melody. The very inner spirit and essence of all wind-songs, bird-songs, passion-songs, folk-songs, country-songs, sex-songs, soul-songs and body-songs hath blown upon me in quick gusts like the breath of passion, and sailed me into a sea of vast dreams, whereof each wave is at once a vision and a melody."

Now fully determined to give himself to music and literature so long as he could keep death at bay, he sought a land of books. Taking his flute and his pen for sword and staff, he turned his face northward. After visiting New York he made his home in Baltimore, December, 1873, under engagement as first flute for the Peabody Symphony Concerts.

With his settlement in Baltimore begins a story of as brave and sad a struggle as the history of genius records. On the one hand was the opportunity for study, and the full consciousness of power, and a will never subdued ; and on the other a body wasting with consumption, that must be forced to task beyond its strength not merely to express the thoughts of beauty which strove for utterance, but from the necessity of providing bread for his babes. His father would have had him return to Macon, and settle down with him in business and share his income, but that would have been the suicide of every duty and ambition. So he wrote from Baltimore to his father, November 29, 1873 :

" I have given your last letter the fullest and most careful consideration. After doing so I feel sure that Macon is not the place for me. If you could taste the delicious crystalline air, and the champagne breeze that I've just been rushing about in, I am equally sure that in point of climate you would agree with me that my chance for life is ten times as great here as in Macon. Then, as to business, why should I, nay, how *can* I, settle myself down to be a third-rate struggling lawyer for the balance of my little life, as long as there is a certainty almost absolute that I can do some other thing so much better? Several persons, from whose judgment in such matters there can be no appeal, have told me, for instance, that I am the greatest flute-player in the world ; and several others, of equally authoritative judgment, have given me an almost equal encouragement to work with my pen (Of course I protest against the necessity which makes me write such things about myself. I only do so because I so appreciate the love and tenderness which prompt you to desire me with you that I will make the fullest explanation possible of my course, out of reciprocal honor and respect for the motives which lead you to think differently from me.) My dear father, think how, for twenty years, through poverty, through pain, through weariness, through sickness, through the uncongenial atmosphere of a farcical college and of a bare army and then of an exacting business life, through all the discouragement of being wholly unacquainted with literary people and literary ways—I say, think how, in spite of all these depressing circumstances, and of a thousand more which I could enumerate, these two figures of music and of poetry have steadily kept in my heart so that I could not banish them. Does it not seem to you as to me, that I begin to have the right to enroll myself among the devotees of these two sublime arts, after having followed them so long and so humbly, and through so much bitterness?"

What could his father do but yield? And what could he do during the following years of his son's fight for standing-room on the planet but help? But for that help, generously given by his father and brother, as their ability allowed, at the critical times of utter prostration, the end would not have been long delayed. For the little that was necessary to give his household a humble support it was not easy for the most strenuous young author to win by his pen in the intervals between his hemorrhages. He asked for very little, only the supply of absolute necessities, what it would be easy for a well man to earn, but what it was very hard for a man to earn scarce able to leave his bed, dependent on the chance income had from poems and articles in magazines that would take them, or from courses of lectures in schools. Often for months together he could do no work. He was driven to Texas, to Florida, to Pennsylvania, to North Carolina, to try to recover health from pine breaths and clover blossoms. Supported by the implicit faith of one heart, which fully believed in his genius, and was willing to wait if he could only find his opportunity, his courage never failed. He still kept before himself first his ideal and his mission, and he longed to live that he might accomplish them. It must have been in such a mood that, soon after coming to Baltimore, he wrote to his wife, who was detained in the South :

"So many great ideas for Art are born to me each day, I am swept away into the land of All-Delight by their strenuous sweet whirlwind ; and I find within myself such entire, yet humble, confidence of possessing every single element of power to carry them all out, save the little paltry sum of money that would suffice to keep us clothed and fed in the meantime.

"I do not understand this."

Lanier's was an unknown name, and he would write only in obedience to his own sense of art, and he did not fit his wares to the taste of those who buy verse. It was to comfort his wife, in this period of greatest uncertainty whether he had not erred in launching in the sea of literature, that he wrote again a letter of frankest confession :

"I will make to thee a little confession of faith, telling thee, my dearer self, in words, what I do not say to my not-so-dear-self except in more modest feeling.

"Know, then, that disappointments were inevitable, and will still come until I have fought the battle which every great artist has had to fight since time began. This—dimly felt while I was doubtful of my own vocation and powers—is clear as the sun to me now that I *know*, through the fiercest tests of life, that I am in soul, and shall be in life and utterance, a great poet.

"The philosophy of my disappointments is, that there is so much *cleverness* standing betwixt me and the public . . . Richard Wagner is sixty years old and over, and one-half of the most cultivated artists of the most cultivated art-land, *quoad* music, still think him an absurdity. Says Schumann in one of his letters : 'The publishers will not listen to me for a moment' ; and dost thou not remember Schubert, and Richter, and John Keats, and a sweet host more ?

"Now this is written because I sit here in my room daily, and picture *thee* picturing *me* worn, and troubled, or disheartened ; and because I do not wish thee to think up any groundless sorrow in thy soul. Of course I have my keen sorrows, momentarily more keen than I would like any one to know; but I thank God that in a knowledge of Him and of myself which cometh to me daily in fresh revelations, I have a steadfast firmament of blue, in which all clouds soon dissolve. I have wanted to say this several times of late, but it is not easy to bring one's self to talk so of one's self, even to one's dearer self.

"Have then . . . no fears nor anxieties in my behalf ; look upon all my disappointments as mere witnesses that art has no enemy so unrelenting as cleverness, and as rough weather that seasons timber. It is of little consequence whether *I* fail ; the *I* in the matter is a small business : ' *Que mon nom soit flétri, que la France soit libre !* ' quoth Danton ; which is to say, interpreted by my environment : Let my name perish—the poetry is good poetry and the music is good music, and beauty dieth not, and the heart that needs it will find it."

Having now given sacredly to art what vital forces his will could command, he devoted himself, with an intense energy, to the study of English literature, making himself a master of Anglo-Saxon and early English texts, and pursuing the study down to our own times. He read freely, also, and with a scholar's nice eagerness, in further fields of study, but all with a view to gathering the stores which a full man might draw from in the practice of poetic art ; for he had that large compass which sees and seeks truths in various excursions, and no field of history, or philology, or philosophy, or science found him unsympathetic. The opportunity for these studies opened a new era in his development, while we begin to find a crystallization of that theory of formal verse which he adopted, and a growing power to master it. To this artistic side of poetry he gave, from this time, very special study, until he had formulated it in his lectures in the Johns Hopkins University, and in his volume " The Science of English Verse."

But from this time the struggle against his fatal disease was conscious and constant. In May, 1874, he visited Florida under an engagement to write a book for distribution by a railroad company. Two months of the summer were spent with his family at Sunnyside, Ga., where "Corn" was written. This poem, published in *Lippincott's Magazine*, was much copied, and made him known to many admirers. No one of these was of so much value to him as Bayard Taylor, at whose suggestion he was chosen to write the cantata for the opening of the Centennial Exposition at Philadelphia, and with whom he carried on a correspondence so long as Mr. Taylor lived. To Mr. Taylor he owed introductions of value to other writers, and for his sympathy and aid his letters prove that he felt very grateful. In his first letter to Mr. Taylor, written August 7, 1875, he says :

"I could never describe to you what a mere drought and famine my life has been, as regards that multitude of matters which I fancy one absorbs when one is in an atmosphere of art, or when one is in conversational relation with men of letters, with travellers, with persons who have either seen, or written, or done large things. Perhaps you know that, with us of the younger generation in the South since the war, pretty much the whole of life has been merely not dying."

The selection of Mr. Lanier to write the Centennial Cantata first brought his name into general notice ; but its publication, in advance of the music by Dudley Buck, was the occasion of an immense amount of ridicule, more or less good-humored. It was written by a musician to go with music under the new relations of poetry to music brought about by the great modern development of the orchestra, and was not to be judged without its orchestral accompaniment. The criticism it received pained our poet, but did not at all affect his faith in his theories of art. To his father he wrote from New York, May 8, 1876 :

"My experience in the varying judgments given about poetry . . . has all converged upon one solitary principle, and the experience of the artist in all ages is reported by history to be of precisely the same direction. That principle is, that the artist shall put forth, humbly and lovingly, and without bitterness against opposition, the very best and highest that is within him, utterly regardless of contemporary criticism. What possible claim can contemporary criticism set up to respect—that criticism which crucified Jesus Christ, stoned Stephen, hooted Paul for a madman, tried Luther for a criminal, tortured Galileo, bound Columbus in chains, drove Dante into a hell of exile, made Shakspere write the sonnet, 'When in disgrace with fortune and men's eyes,' gave Milton five pounds for ' Paradise Lost,' kept Samuel Johnson cooling his heels on Lord Chesterfield's doorstep, reviled Shelley as an unclean dog killed Keats, cracked jokes on Glück, Schubert, Beethoven, Berlioz, and Wagner, and committed so many other impious follies and stupidities that a thousand letters like this could not suffice even to catalogue them ?"

Since first coming to the North in September, 1873, Mr. Lanier had been separated from his family. The two happy months with them after his visit to Florida was followed by several other briefer visits. The winters of 1874-75 and 1875-76 found him still in Baltimore, playing at the Peabody, pursuing his studies and writing the "Symphony," the 'Psalm of the West," the "Cantata," and some shorter poems, with a series of prose descriptive articles for *Lippincott's Magazine.* In the summer of 1876 he called his family to join him at West Chester, Pa. This was authorized by an engagement to write the Life of Charlotte Cushman. The work was begun, but the engagement was broken two months later, owing to the illness of the friend of the family who was to provide the material from the mass of private correspondence.

Following this disappointment a new cold was incurred, and his health became so much impaired that in November the physicians told him he could not expect to live longer than May, unless he sought a warmer climate. About the middle of December he started with his wife for the Gulf coast, and visited Tampa, Fla., gaining considerable benefit from the mild climate. In April he ventured North again, tarrying through the spring with his friends in Georgia ; and, after a summer with his own family in Chadd's Ford, Pa., a final move was ventured in October to Baltimore as home. Here he resumed his old place in the Peabody orchestra, and continued to play there for three winters.

The Old English studies which he had pursued with such deep delight, he now put to use in a course of lectures on Elizabethan Verse, given in a private parlor to a class of thirty ladies. This was followed by a more ambitious "Shakspere Course" of lectures in the smaller hall of the Peabody Institute. The undertaking was immensely cheered on and greatly praised, but was a financial failure. It opened the way, however, to one of the chiefest delights of his life, his appointment as lecturer on English literature for the ensuing year at the Johns Hopkins University. After some correspondence on the subject with President Gilman, he received notice on his birthday, 1879, of his appointment, with a salary attached (it may be mentioned), which gave him the first income assured in any year since his marriage. This stimulated him to new life, for he was now barely able to walk after a severe illness and renewed hemorrhage.

The last two years had been more fruitful in verse than any that had gone before, as he had now acquired confidence in his view of the principles of art. In 1875 he had written :

"In this little song ['Special Pleading'] I have begun to dare to give myself some freedom in my own peculiar style, and have allowed myself to treat words, similes, and metres with such freedom as I desired. The result convinces me that I can do so now safely."

Among his poems of this period may be mentioned "A Song of the Future," "The Revenge of Hamish," and—what are excellent examples of the kind of art of which he had now gained command —"The Song of the Chattahoochee," and "A Song of Love." It was at this time that he wrote "The Marshes of Glynn," his most ambitious poem thus far, and one which he intended to follow with a series of "Hymns of the Marshes," which he left incomplete.

The summer of 1879 was spent at Rockingham Springs, Va., and here, in six weeks, was begun and finished his volume, "Science of English Verse." Another severe illness prostrated him in September, but the necessity of work allowed no time for such distractions. In October he opened three lecture courses in young ladies' schools ; and through the winter, notwithstanding a most menacing illness about January 1st, he was in continuous rehearsals and concerts at the Peabody, and besides miscellaneous writings and studies, gave weekly ten lectures upon English literature, two of them public at the University, two to University classes, and the remaining six at private schools. The University public lectures upon English Verse, more especially Shakspere's, in part contained, and in part were introductory to, " The Science of English Verse."

The final consuming fever opened in May, 1880. In July he went with Mrs. Lanier and her father to West Chester, Pa., where a fourth son was born in August. Unable to bear the fall climate, he returned, alone, early in September to his Baltimore home.

This winter brought a hand-to-hand battle for life. In December he came to the very door of death. Before February he had essayed the open air to test himself for his second University lecture course. His improvement ceased on that first day of exposure. Nevertheless, by April he had gone through the twelve lectures (there were to have been twenty), which were later published under the title " The English Novel." A few of tne earlier lectures he penned himself ; the rest he was obliged to dictate to his wife. With the utmost care of himself, going in a closed carriage and sitting during his lecture, his strength was so exhausted that the struggle for breath in the carriage on his return seemed each time to threaten the end. Those who heard him listened with a sort of fascinated terror, as in doubt whether the hoarded breath would suffice to the end of the hour.

It was in December of this winter, when too feeble to raise his food to his mouth, with a fever temperature of 104 degrees, that he pencilled his last and greatest poem, " Sunrise," one of his projected series of the " Hymns of the Marshes." It seemed as if he were in fear that he would die with it unuttered.

At the end of April, 1881, he made his last visit to New York, to complete arrangements with Charles Scribner's Sons for the publication of other books of the King Arthur series. But in a day or two aggravated illness compelled his wife to join him, and his medical adviser pronounced tent-life in a pure, high climate to be the last hope. His brother Clifford was summoned from Alabama to assist in carrying out the plans for encamping near Asheville, N. C., whither the brothers went soon after the middle of May. By what seemed a hopeful coincidence he was tendered a commission to write an account of the region in a railroad interest, as he had done six years before with Florida. This provided a monthly salary, which was to be the dependence of himself and family. The materials for this book were collected, and the book thoroughly shaped in the author's mind when July ended ; but his increasing anguish kept him from dictating, often from all speech for hours, and he carried the plan away with him.

A site was chosen on the side of Richmond Hill, three miles from Asheville. Clifford returned to Alabama, after seeing the tents pitched and floored, and Mrs. Lanier came with her infant to take her place as nurse for the invalid. Early in July Mr. Lanier the father, with his wife, joined them in the encampment. As the passing weeks brought no improvement to the sufferer he started, August 4th, on a carriage journey across the mountains with his wife, to test the climate of Lynn, Polk County, N. C. There a deadly illness attacked him. No return was possible, and Clifford was summoned by telegraph, and assisted his father in removing the encampment to Lynn. Deceived by hope, and pressed by business cares, Clifford went home August 24th, and the father and his wife five days later, expecting to return soon. Mrs. Lanier's own words, as written in the brief "annals" of his life furnished me, will tell the end :

"We are left alone " (August 29th) "with one another. On the last night of the summer comes a change. His love and immortal will hold off the destroyer of our summer yet one more week, until the forenoon of September 7th, and then falls the frost, and that unfaltering will renders its supreme submission to the adored will of God."

So the tragedy ended, the manly struggle carried on with indomitable resolution against illness and want and care. Just when he seemed to have conquered success enough to assure him a little leisure to write his poems, then his feeble but resolute hold upon earth was exhausted. What he left behind him was written with his life-blood. High above all the evils of the world he lived in a realm of ideal serenity, as if it were the business of life to conquer difficulties.

This is not the place for an essay on the genius of Sidney Lanier. It is enough to call attention to some marked points in his character and work.

He had more than Milton's love for music. He

sung like a bard to the accompaniment of a harp. He lived in sweet sounds : forever conscious of a ceaseless flow of melody which, if resisted for awhile by business occupations, would swell again in its natural current and break at his bidding into audible music.

We have the following recognition of his genius from Asger Hamerik, his Director for six years in the Peabody Symphony Orchestra of Baltimore :

" To him as a child in his cradle Music was given : the heavenly gift to feel and to express himself in tones. His human nature was like an enchanted instrument, a magic flute, or the lyre of Apollo, needing but a breath or a touch to send its beauty out into the world. It was indeed irresistible that he should turn with those poetical feelings which transcend language to the penetrating gentleness of the flute, or the infinite passion of the violin ; for there was an agreement, a spiritual correspondence between his nature and theirs, so that they mutually absorbed and expressed each other. In his hands the flute no longer remained a mere material instrument, but was transformed into a voice that set heavenly harmonies into vibration. Its tones developed colors, warmth, and a low sweetness of unspeakable poetry ; they were not only true and pure, but poetic, allegoric as it were, suggestive of the depths and heights of being and of the delights which the earthly ear never hears and the earthly eye never sees. No doubt his firm faith in these lofty idealities gave him the power to present them to our imaginations, and thus by the aid of the higher language of Music to inspire others with that sense of beauty in which he constantly dwelt.

" His conception of music was not reached by an analytic study of note by note, but was intuitive and spontaneous ; like a woman's reason : he felt it so, because he felt it so, and his delicate perception required no more logical form of reasoning.

"His playing appealed alike to the musically learned
and to the unlearned—for he would magnetize the
listener : but the artist felt in his performance the
superiority of the momentary living inspiration to all
the rules and shifts of mere technical scholarship.
His art was not only the art of art, but an art above
art.

"I will never forget the impression he made on me
when he played the flute-concerto of Emil Hartmann
at a Peabody symphony concert, in 1878 : his tall,
handsome, manly presence, his flute breathing noble
sorrows, noble joys, the orchestra softly responding.
The audience was spellbound. Such distinction,
such refinement ! He stood, the master, the genius."

In the one novel which he wrote at the age of
twenty-five, he makes one of his characters say :

"To make a *home* out of a household, given the raw
materials—to wit, wife, children, a friend or two, and
a house—two other things are necessary. These are
a good fire and good music. And inasmuch as we
can do without the fire for half the year, I may say
music is the one essential." "Late explorers say they
have found some nations that have no God; but I
have not read of any that had no music." "Music
means harmony, harmony means love, love means—
God ! "

The theoretical relation between music and poetry
would hardly have attracted his study had it not been
that his mind was as truly philosophically and scien-
tifically accurate, as it was poetically sensuous and
imaginative. In a letter to Mr. E. C. Stedman he
complained that "in all directions the poetic art was
suffering from the shameful circumstance that criti-
cism was without a scientific basis for even the most
elementary of its judgments."

Although the work was irksome to him, he could

not go on writing at hap-hazard, trusting to his own mere taste to decide what was good, until he had settled for himself scientifically what are the laws of poetical construction. This accounts for his exposition of the laws of beauty in that unique work, "The Science of English Verse," which was based on Dante's thought, "The best conceptions cannot be save where science and genius are." The book is chiefly taken up with a discussion of rhythm and tone-color in verse ; and it is well within the truth to say that it is the most complete and thorough original investigation of the formal element in poetry in existence. The rhythm he treated as the marking of definite time measurements, which could be indicated by bars in musical notation, having their regular time and their regular number of notes, with their proper accent. To this time measurement Mr. Lanier gave the pre-eminence which Coleridge and other writers have given to accent. He conceived of a line of poetry as consisting of a definite number of bars (or feet), each bar containing, in dactylic metre, three equal "eighth notes," of which the first is accented, or in iambic metre (which has the same "triple" time), of one "eighth note," and one "quarter note," with the accent on the second. Thus the accented syllable is not necessarily "longer" than the unaccented, except as the rhythm happens to make it so. This idea is very fully developed and with great wealth of curious Old English illustrations. Under the designation of "tone-color" he treats very suggestively of rhyme, alliteration, and vowel and consonant distribution, showing how the recurrence of euphonic vowels and consonants secures that rich variety of tone-color which music gives in orchestration. The work thus

breaks away from the classic grammarian's tables
of trochees and anapæsts, and discusses the forms
of poetry in the terms of music ; and of both tone-
color and of rhythm he would say, in the words of
old King James, "the very touch-stone whereof is
music."

Illustrations of these technical beauties of musical
rhythm, and vowel and consonant distribution, abound
in Lanier's poetry.   Such is the "Song of the Chat-
tahoochee," which deserves a place beside Tennyson's
"Brook."   It strikes a higher key, and is scarcely
less musical.   Such passages are numerous in his
"Sunrise on the Marshes," as in the lines beginning,

"Not slower than majesty moves,"

or the other lines beginning,

"Oh, what if a sound should be made !"

These investigations in the science of verse bore
their fruit especially in the poems written during the
last three or four years of his life, when his sense of
the solemn sacredness of Art became more profound,
and he acquired a greater ease in putting into prac-
tice his theory of verse.   And this made him thor-
oughly original.   He was no imitator either of Tenny-
son or of Swinburne, though musically he is nearer
to them than to any others of his day.   We constantly
notice in his verse that dainty effect which the ear
loves, and which comes from deft marshalling of
consonants and vowels, so that they shall add their
suppler and subtler reinforcement to the steady in-
fantry tramp of rhythm.   Of this delicate art, which
is much more than mere alliteration, which is con-
cerned with dominant accented vowels as well as con-
sonants, with the easy flow of liquids and fricatives,

and with the progressive opening or closing of the organs of articulation, the laws are not easy to formulate, but examples abound in Lanier's poems.

Mr. Stedman, poet and critic, raises the question whether Lanier's extreme conjunction of the artistic with the poetic temperament, which he says no man has more clearly displayed, did not somewhat hamper and delay his power of adequate expression. Possibly, but he was building not for the day, but for time. He must work out his laws of poetry, even if he had almost to invent its language ; for to him was given the power of analysis as well as of construction, and he was too conscientious to do anything else than to find out what was best and why, and then tell and teach it as he had learnt it, even if men said that his late spring was delaying bud and blossom.

But it would be a great mistake to find in Lanier only, or chiefly, the artist. He had the substance of poetry. He possessed both elements, as Stedman says, " in extreme conjunction." He overflowed with fancy. His imagination needed to be held in check. This was recognized in " Corn," and appears more fully in " The Symphony," the first productions which gave him wide recognition as a poet. Illustrations too much abound to allow selection.

And for the substance of invention there needed, in Lanier's judgment, large and exact knowledge of the world's facts. A poet must be a student of things, truths, and men. His own studies were wide and his scholarship accurate. He did not believe that art comes all by instinct, without work. In one of his keen criticisms of poets he said of Edgar A. Poe, whom he esteemed more highly than his countrymen are wont to do : " The trouble with Poe was, he did not *know* enough.   He needed to know a good many more things in order to be a great poet."   Lanier had "a passion for the exact truth," and all of it.

The intense sacredness with which Lanier invested Art held him thrall to the highest ethical ideas.   To him the most beautiful thing of all was Right.   He loved the words, "the beauty of holiness," and it pleased him to reverse the phrase and call it "the holiness of beauty."   When one reads Lanier, he is reminded of two writers, Milton and Ruskin.   More than any other great English authors they are dominated by this beauty of holiness.   Lanier was saturated with it.   It shines out of every line he wrote.   It is not that he never wrote a maudlin line, but that every thought was lofty.   That it must be so was a first postulate of his Art.   Hear his words to the students of Johns Hopkins University :

"Let any sculptor hew us out the most ravishing combination of tender curves and spheric softness that ever stood for woman ; yet if the lip have a certain fulness that hints of the flesh, if the brow be insincere, if in the minutest particular the physical beauty suggest a moral ugliness, that sculptor—unless he be portraying a moral ugliness for a moral purpose—may as well give over his marble for paving-stones.   Time, whose judgments are inexorably moral, will not accept his work.   For, indeed, we may say that he who has not yet perceived how artistic beauty and moral beauty are convergent lines which run back into a common ideal origin, and who therefore is not afire with moral beauty just as with artistic beauty—that he, in short, who has not come to that stage of quiet and eternal frenzy in which the beauty of holiness and the holiness of beauty mean one thing, burn as one fire, shine as one light within him ; he is not yet the great artist."

And he returns to the theme :

"Can not one say with authority to the young artist, whether working in stone, in color, in tones, or in character-forms of the novel : So far from dreading that your moral purpose will interfere with your beautiful creation, go forward in the clear conviction that unless you are suffused—soul and body, one might say—with that moral purpose which finds its largest expression in love ; that is, the love of all things in their proper relation ; unless you are suffused with this love, do not dare to meddle with beauty ; unless you are suffused with beauty, do not dare to meddle with love ; unless you are suffused with truth, do not dare to meddle with goodness ; in a word, unless you are suffused with truth, wisdom, goodness, and love, abandon the hope that the ages will accept you as an artist."

Thus was it true, as was said of his work by his associate, Dr. Wm. Hand Browne, that "one thread of purpose runs through it all. This thread is found in his fervid love for his fellow-men, and his never ceasing endeavors to kindle an enthusiasm for beauty, purity, nobility of life, which he held it the poet's first duty to teach and to exemplify." And so there came into his verse a solemn, worshipful element, dominating it everywhere, and giving loftiness to its beauty. For he was the democrat whom he described in contrast to Whitman's mere brawny, six-footed, open-shirted hero, whose strength was only that of the biceps:

"My democrat, the democrat whom I contemplate with pleasure, the democrat who is to write or to read the poetry of the future, may have a mere thread for his biceps, yet he shall be strong enough to handle hell ; he shall play ball with the earth ; and albeit his stature may be no more than a boy's, he shall still be taller than the great redwoods of California; his height shall be the height of great resolution, and love, and faith, and beauty, and knowledge, and subtle meditation; his head shall be forever among the stars."

This standard he could not forget in his judgments of artists. There was something in Whitman which "refreshed him like harsh salt spray," but to Whitman's lawlessness of art he was an utter foe. We find it written down in his notes:

"Whitman is poetry's butcher. Huge raw collops slashed from the rump of poetry, and never mind gristle—is what Whitman feeds our souls with."

"As near as I can make it out, Whitman's argument seems to be, that, because a prairie is wide, therefore debauchery is admirable, and because the Mississippi is long, therefore every American is God."

So he says of Swinburne:

"He invited me to eat; the service was silver and gold, but no food therein save pepper and salt."

And of William Morris:

"He caught a crystal cupful of the yellow light of sunset, and persuading himself to dream it wine, drank it with a sort of smile."

Though not what would be called a religious writer, Lanier's large and deep thought took him to the deepest spiritual faiths, and the vastness of Nature drew him to a trust in the Infinite above us. Thus, his young search after God and truth brought him into the membership of the Presbyterian Church while at Oglethorpe College; and though in after years his creed became broader than that imposed by the Church he had joined on its clergy, he could not outgrow the simple faith and consecration which are all it requires of its membership.   His college note-book records his earnestness ;

" Liberty, patriotism, and civilization are on their knees before the men of the South, and with clasped hands and straining eyes are begging them to become Christians."

How naturally his large faith in God finds expression in his " Marshes of Glynn ; " or his reverent discipleship of the great Artist and Master in his " Ballad of the Trees and the Master," or his " The Crystal," which was Christ.   Yet, with not a whit less of worshipfulness and consecration, there grew in him a repugnance to the sectarianism of the Churches which put him somewhat out of sympathy with their formal organizations.   He wrote, in what may have been a sketch for a poem :

"I fled in tears from the men's ungodly quarrel about God.   I fled in tears to the woods, and laid me down on the earth.   Then somewhat like the beating of many hearts came up to me out of the ground ; and I looked and my cheek lay close to a violet.   Then my heart took courage, and I said :
' I know that thou art the word of my God, dear Violet :
And Oh, the ladder is not long that to my heaven leads.
Measure what space a violet stands above the ground
'Tis no further climbing that my soul and angels have to do than that.' "

It was this quality, high and consecrate, as of a palmer with his vow, this knightly valiance, this constant San Greal quest after the lofty in character and aim, this passion for Good and Love, which fellows him rather with Milton and Ruskin than with the less sturdily built poets of his day, and which puts him in sharpest contrast with the school led by Swinburne—with Rossetti and Morris as his followers hard after him—a school whose reed has a short gamut, and plays but two notes, Mors and Eros, hopeless death and lawless love. But poetry is larger and finer than they know. Its face is toward the world's future; it does not maunder after the flower-decked nymphs and yellow-skirted fays that have forever fled —and good riddance—their haunted springs and tangled thickets. It can feed on its growing sweet and fresh faiths, but will draw foul contagion from the rank mists that float over old and cold fables. For all knowledge is food, as faith is wine, to a genius like Lanier. A poet genius has great common sense. He lives in to-day and to-morrow, not in yesterday. Such men were Shakspere and Goethe. The age of poetry is not past; there is nothing in culture or science hostile to it. Milton was one of the world's great poets, but he was the most cultured and scholarly and statesmanlike man of his day. He was no dreamer of dead dreams. Neither was Lanier a dreamer. He came late to the opportunity he longed for, but when he came to it he was a tremendous student, not of music alone, but of language, of philosophy, and of science. He loved science. He was an inventor. He had all the instincts and ambitions of this nineteenth century. But that only made his range of poetic thought wider as his outlook became larger. The world is opening to the poet with every question the crucible asks of the elements, with every spectrum the prism steals from a star. The old he has and all the new.

All this a man of Lanier's breadth understood fully, for he had a large capacity and he sought a full equipment. Perhaps the most remarkable feature of his gifts was their complete symmetry. It is hard to tell what register of perception, or sensibility, or wit, or will was lacking. The constructive and the critical faculties, the imaginative and the practical, balanced each other. His wit and humor played upon the soberer background of his more recognized qualities. The artist's withdrawn vision was at any need promptly exchanged for the exercise of that scrupulous exactitude called for in the routine of the law-office or the post-office clerkship or other business relations, or for the play of those energies exerted in camp or field. There, so his comrades testify, the most wearing drudgeries of a soldier's life were always undertaken with notable alacrity and were thoroughly discharged, when he would as invariably return, the task being done, to the gentle region of his own high thoughts and the artist's realm of beauty.

But how short was his day, and how slender his opportunity! From the time he was of age he waged a constant, courageous, hopeless fight against adverse circumstance for room to live and write. Much very dear, and sweet, and most sympathetic helpfulness he met in the city of his adoption, and from friends elsewhere, but he could not command the time and leisure which might have lengthened his life and given him opportunity to write the music and the verse with which his soul was teeming. Yet short as was his literary life, and hindered though it were, its fruit will fill a large space in the garnering of the poetic art of our country.

WILLIAM HAYES WARD.

Mr. Lanier's published works, previous to the present volume, and exclusive of poems and essays published in literary journals, are the following :

TIGER LILIES : A novel. 16 mo, pp. v, 252. Hurd & Houghton, New York, 1867.

FLORIDA : Its Scenery, Climate and History. 12 mo, pp. 336. J. B. Lippincott & Co., Philadelphia, 1876.

POEMS. Pp. 94. J. B. Lippincott & Co., Philadelphia, 1877.

THE BOY'S FROISSART. Being Sir John Froissart's Chronicles of Adventure, Battle, and Custom in England, France, Spain, etc. Edited for Boys. Crown 8vo, pp. xxviii 422. Charles Scribner's Sons, New York, 1878.

THE SCIENCE OF ENGLISH VERSE. Crown 8vo, pp. xv, 315. Charles Scribner's Sons, New York, 1880.

THE BOY'S KING ARTHUR. Being Sir Thomas Malory's History of King Arthur and his Knights of the Round Table. Edited for Boys. Crown 8vo, pp. xlviii, 404. Charles Scribner's Sons, New York, 1880.

THE BOY'S MABINOGION. Being the Earliest Welsh Tales of King Arthur in the famous Red Book of Hergest. Edited for Boys. Crown 8vo, pp. xxiv, 378. Charles Scribner's Sons, New York, 1881.

THE BOY'S PERCY. Being Old Ballads of War, Adventure, and Love, from Bishop Thomas Percy's Reliques of Ancient English Poetry. Edited for Boys. Crown 8vo, pp. xxxii, 442. Charles Scribner's Sons, New York, 1882.

THE ENGLISH NOVEL AND THE PRINCIPLES OF ITS DEVELOPMENT. Crown 8vo, pp. 293. Charles Scribner's Sons, New York, 1883.

POEMS OF SIDNEY LANIER

SUNRISE, *the culminating poem, the high-est vision of Sidney Lanier, was dedicated through his latest request to that friend who indeed came into his life only near its close, yet was at first meeting recognized by the poet as "the father of his spirit,"* GEORGE WESTFELDT. *When words were very few and the poem was unread, even by any friend, the earnest bidding came: "Send him my* SUNRISE, *that he may know how entirely we are one in thought."*

HYMNS OF THE MARSHES.

I.

SUNRISE.

In my sleep I was fain of their fellowship, fain
  Of the live-oak, the marsh, and the main.
The little green leaves would not let me alone in my sleep ;
Up-breathed from the marshes, a message of range and of
      sweep,
Interwoven with waftures of wild sea-liberties, drifting,
  Came through the lapped leaves sifting, sifting,
      Came to the gates of sleep.
Then my thoughts, in the dark of the dungeon-keep
Of the Castle of Captives hid in the City of Sleep,
Upstarted, by twos and by threes assembling :
  The gates of sleep fell a-trembling
Like as the lips of a lady that forth falter *yes*,
      Shaken with happiness :
  The gates of sleep stood wide.

I have waked, I have come, my beloved ! I might not abide :
I have come ere the dawn, O beloved, my live-oaks, to hide
      In your gospelling glooms,—to be
As a lover in heaven, the marsh my marsh and the sea my sea.

Tell me, sweet burly-bark'd, man-bodied Tree
That mine arms in the dark are embracing, dost know
From what fount are these tears at thy feet which flow ?

They rise not from reason, but deeper inconsequent deeps.
     Reason's not one that weeps.
    What logic of greeting lies
Betwixt dear over-beautiful trees and the rain of the eyes ?

O cunning green leaves, little masters ! like as ye gloss
All the dull-tissued dark with your luminous darks that em-
     boss
The vague blackness of night into pattern and plan,
            So,
   (But would I could know, but would I could know,)
With your question embroid'ring the dark of the question of
     man,—
So, with your silences purfling this silence of man
While his cry to the dead for some knowledge is under the
     ban,
         Under the ban,—
    So, ye have wrought me
Designs on the night of our knowledge,—yea, ye have taught
     me,
           So,
   That haply we know somewhat more than we know.

     Ye lispers, whisperers, singers in storms,
     Ye consciences murmuring faiths under forms,
     Ye ministers meet for each passion that grieves,
     Friendly, sisterly, sweetheart leaves,
Oh, rain me down from your darks that contain me
Wisdoms ye winnow from winds that pain me,—
Sift down tremors of sweet-within-sweet
That advise me of more than they bring,—repeat
Me the woods-smell that swiftly but now brought breath
From the heaven-side bank of the river of death,—
   Teach me the terms of silence,—preach me
   The passion of patience,—sift me,—impeach me,—

And there, oh there
As ye hang with your myriad palms upturned in the air,
Pray me a myriad prayer.

My gossip, the owl,—is it thou
That out of the leaves of the low-hanging bough,
As I pass to the beach, art stirred?
Dumb woods, have ye uttered a bird?

*   *   *   *   *   *   *   *

Reverend Marsh, low-couched along the sea,
Old chemist, rapt in alchemy,
Distilling silence,—lo,
That which our father-age had died to know—
The menstruum that dissolves all matter—thou
Hast found it : for this silence, filling now
The globéd charity of receiving space,
This solves us all : man, matter, doubt, disgrace,
Death, love, sin, sanity,
Must in yon silence, clear solution lie.
Too clear !   That crystal nothing who'll peruse ?
The blackest night could bring us brighter news.
Yet precious qualities of silence haunt
Round these vast margins, ministrant.
Oh, if thy soul's at latter gasp for space,
With trying to breathe no bigger than thy race
Just to be fellow'd, when that thou hast found
No man with room, or grace enough of bound
To entertain that New thou tell'st, thou art,—
'Tis here, 'tis here, thou canst unhand thy heart
And breathe it free, and breathe it free,
By rangy marsh, in lone sea-liberty.

The tide's at full: the marsh with flooded streams
Glimmers, a limpid labyrinth of dreams.

Each winding creek in grave entrancement lies
A rhapsody of morning-stars.   The skies
Shine scant with one forked galaxy,—
The marsh brags ten : looped on his breast they lie.

Oh, what if a sound should be made !
Oh, what if a bound should be laid
To this bow-and-string tension of beauty and silence a-
      spring,—
To the bend of beauty the bow, or the hold of silence the
      string !
I fear me. I fear me yon dome of diaphanous gleam
Will break as a bubble o'er-blown in a dream,—
Yon dome of too-tenuous tissues of space and of night,
Over-weighted with stars, over-freighted with light,
Over-sated with beauty and silence, will seem
   But a bubble that broke in a dream,
If a bound of degree to this grace be laid,
      Or a sound or a motion made.

But no : it is made: list ! somewhere,—mystery, where ?
            In the leaves ? in the air?
In my heart ? is a motion made :
'Tis a motion of dawn, like a flicker of shade on shade.
In the leaves 'tis palpable : low multitudinous stirring
Upwinds through the woods ; the little ones, softly conferring,
Have settled my lord 's to be looked for ; so ; they are still;
But the air and my heart and the earth are a-thrill,—
And look where the wild duck sails round the bend of the
      river,—
   And look where a passionate shiver
   Expectant is bending the blades
Ot the marsh-grass in serial shimmers and shades,—
And invisible wings, fast fleeting, fast fleeting,
            Are beating

The dark overhead as my heart beats,—and steady and
    free
Is the ebb-tide flowing from marsh to sea—
    (Run home, little streams,
    With your lapfulls of stars and dreams),—
And a sailor unseen is hoisting a-peak,
For list, down the inshore curve of the creek
    How merrily flutters the sail,—
And lo, in the East! Will the East unveil?
The East is unveiled, the East hath confessed
A flush: 'tis dead; 'tis alive: 'tis dead, ere the West
Was aware of it: nay, 'tis abiding, 'tis unwithdrawn:
    Have a care, sweet Heaven! 'Tis Dawn.

Now a dream of a flame through that dream of a flush is up-
    rolled:
    To the zenith ascending, a dome of undazzling gold
Is builded, in shape as a bee-hive, from out of the sea:
The hive is of gold undazzling, but oh, the Bee,
    The star-fed Bee, the build-fire Bee,
    Of dazzling gold is the great Sun-Bee
That shall flash from the hive-hole over the sea.

    Yet now the dew-drop, now the morning gray,
    Shall live their little lucid sober day
    Ere with the sun their souls exhale away.
Now in each pettiest personal sphere of dew
The summ'd moon shines complete as in the blue
Big dew-drop of all heaven: with these lit shrines
O'er-silvered to the farthest sea-confines,
The sacramental marsh one pious plain
Of worship lies. Peace to the ante-reign
Of Mary Morning, blissful mother mild,
Minded of nought but peace, and of a child.

Not slower than Majesty moves, for a mean and a measure
Of motion,—not faster than dateless Olympian leisure
Might pace with unblown ample garments from pleasure to
     pleasure,—
The wave-serrate sea-rim sinks unjarring, unreeling,
    Forever revealing, revealing, revealing,
Edgewise, bladewise, halfwise, wholewise,—'tis done !
         Good-morrow, lord Sun !
With several voice, with ascription one,
The woods and the marsh and the sea and my soul
Unto thee, whence the glittering stream of all morrows doth
    roll,
Cry good and past-good and most heavenly morrow, lord
    Sun.

O Artisan born in the purple,—Workman Heat,—
Parter of passionate atoms that travail to meet,
And be mixed in the death-cold oneness,—innermost Guest
At the marriage of elements,—fellow of publicans,—blest
King in the blouse of flame, that loiterest o'er
The idle skies yet laborest fast evermore,—
Thou, in the fine forge-thunder, thou, in the beat
Of the heart of a man, thou Motive,—Laborer Heat :
Yea, Artist, thou, of whose art yon sea 's all news,
With his inshore greens and manifold mid-sea blues,
Pearl-glint, shell-tint, ancientest perfectest hues
Ever shaming the maidens,—lily and rose
Confess thee, and each mild flame that glows
In the clarified virginal bosoms of stones that shine,
        It is thine, it is thine :

Thou chemist of storms, whether driving the winds a-swirl
Or a-flicker the subtiler essences polar that whirl
In the magnet earth,—yea, thou with a storm for a heart,
Rent with debate, many-spotted with question, part

From part oft sundered, yet ever a globéd light,
Yet ever the artist, ever more large and bright
Than the eye of a man may avail of:—manifold One,
I must pass from the face, I must pass from the face of the
      Sun :
Old Want is awake and agog, every wrinkle a-frown ;
The worker must pass to his work in the terrible town :
But I fear not, nay, and I fear not the thing to be done ;
  I am strong with the strength of my lord the Sun :
How dark, how dark soever the race that must needs be run,
      I am lit with the Sun.

Oh, never the mast-high run of the seas
      Of traffic shall hide thee,
Never the hell-colored smoke of the factories
      Hide thee,
Never the reek of the time's fen-politics
      Hide thee,
And ever my heart through the night shall with knowledge
    abide thee,
And ever by day shall my spirit, as one that hath tried thee,
  Labor, at leisure, in art,—till yonder beside thee
    My soul shall float, friend Sun,
      The day being done.

BALTIMORE, December, 1880.
   1*

II.

INDIVIDUALITY.

SAIL on, sail on, fair cousin Cloud :
Oh loiter hither from the sea.
　　Still-eyed and shadow-brow'd,
Steal off from yon far-drifting crowd,
And come and brood upon the marsh with me.

Yon laboring low horizon-smoke,
Yon stringent sail, toil not for thee
　　Nor me ; did heaven's stroke
The whole deep with drown'd commerce choke,
No pitiless tease of risk or bottomry

Would to thy rainy office close
Thy will, or lock mine eyes from tears,
　　Part wept for traders'-woes,
Part for that ventures mean as those
In issue bind such sovereign hopes and fears.

—Lo, Cloud, thy downward countenance stares
Blank on the blank-faced marsh, and thou
　　Mindest of dark affairs ;
Thy substance seems a warp of cares ;
Like late wounds run the wrinkles on thy brow.

Well may'st thou pause, and gloom, and stare,
A visible conscience : I arraign
　　Thee, criminal Cloud, of rare
Contempts on Mercy, Right, and Prayer,—
Of murders, arsons, thefts,—of nameless stain.

(Yet though life's logic grow as gray
As thou, my soul's not in eclipse.)
    Cold Cloud, but yesterday
Thy lightning slew a child at play,
And then a priest with prayers upon his lips

For his enemies, and then a bright
Lady that did but ope the door
    Upon the storming night
To let a beggar in,—strange spite,—
And then thy sulky rain refused to pour

Till thy quick torch a barn had burned
Where twelve months' store of victual lay,
    A widow's sons had earned ;
Which done, thy floods with winds returned,—
The river raped their little herd away.

What myriad righteous errands high
Thy flames *might* run on !   In that hour
    Thou slewest the child, oh why
Not rather slay Calamity,
Breeder of Pain and Doubt, infernal Power ?

Or why not plunge thy blades about
Some maggot politician throng
    Swarming to parcel out
The body of a land, and rout
The maw-conventicle, and ungorge Wrong ?

> *What the cloud doeth*
> *The Lord knoweth,*
> *The cloud knoweth not.*
> *What the artist doeth,*
> *The Lord knoweth ;*
> *Knoweth the artist not ?*

Well-answered !—O dear artists, ye
—Whether in forms of curve or hue
   Or tone your gospels be—
Say wrong *This work is not of me*,
But God : it is not true, it is not true.

Awful is Art because 'tis free.
The artist trembles o'er his plan
   Where men his Self must see,
Who made a song or picture, he
Did it, and not another, God nor man.

My Lord is large, my Lord is strong :
Giving, He gave : my me is mine.
   How poor, how strange, how wrong,
To dream He wrote the little song
I made to Him with love's unforced design !

Oh, not as clouds dim laws have plann'd
To strike down Good and fight for Ill,—
   Oh, not as harps that stand
In the wind and sound the wind's command :
Each artist—gift of terror !—owns his will.

For thee, Cloud,—if thou spend thine all
Upon the South's o'er-brimming sea
   That needs thee not ; or crawl
To the dry provinces, and fall
Till every convert clod shall give to thee

Green worship ; if thou grow or fade,
Bring on delight or misery,
   Fly east or west, be made
Snow, hail, rain, wind, grass, rose, light, shade ;
What matters it to thee ?   There is no thee.

Pass, kinsman Cloud, now fair and mild :
Discharge the will that 's not thine own.
   I work in freedom wild,
But work, as plays a little child,
Sure of the Father, Self, and Love, alone.

BALTIMORE, 1878–9.

III.

MARSH SONG—AT SUNSET.

OVER the monstrous shambling sea,
   Over the Caliban sea,
Bright Ariel-cloud, thou lingerest :
Oh wait, oh wait, in the warm red West,—
   Thy Prospero I 'll be.

Over the humped and fishy sea,
   Over the Caliban sea
O cloud in the West, like a thought in the heart
Of pardon, loose thy wing, and start,
   And do a grace for me.

Over the huge and huddling sea,
   Over the Caliban sea,
Bring hither my brother Antonio,—Man,—
My injurer : night breaks the ban :
   Brother, I pardon thee.

BALTIMORE, 1879–80.

IV.

THE MARSHES OF GLYNN.

GLOOMS of the live-oaks, beautiful-braided and woven
With intricate shades of the vines that myriad-cloven
  Clamber the forks of the multiform boughs,—
          Emerald twilights,—
          Virginal shy lights,
Wrought of the leaves to allure to the whisper of vows,
When lovers pace timidly down through the green colon-
    nades
Of the dim sweet woods, of the dear dark woods,
  Of the heavenly woods and glades,
That run to the radiant marginal sand-beach within
      The wide sea-marshes of Glynn ;—

Beautiful glooms, soft dusks in the noon-day fire,—
Wildwood privacies, closets of lone desire,
Chamber from chamber parted with wavering arras of
    leaves,—
Cells for the passionate pleasure of prayer to the soul that
    grieves,
Pure with a sense of the passing of saints through the wood,
Cool for the dutiful weighing of ill with good ;—

O braided dusks of the oak and woven shades of the vine,
While the riotous noon-day sun of the June-day long did
    shine
Ye held me fast in your heart and I held you fast in mine ;

But now when the noon is no more, and riot is rest,
And the sun is a-wait at the ponderous gate of the West,
And the slant yellow beam down the wood-aisle doth seem
Like a lane into heaven that leads from a dream,—
Ay, now, when my soul all day hath drunken the soul of the
    oak,
And my heart is at ease from men, and the wearisome sound
    of the stroke
  Of the scythe of time and the trowel of trade is low,
  And belief overmasters doubt, and I know that I know,
  And my spirit is grown to a lordly great compass within,
That the length and the breadth and the sweep of the marshes
    of Glynn
Will work me no fear like the fear they have wrought me of
    yore
When length was fatigue, and when breadth was but bitter-
    ness sore,
And when terror and shrinking and dreary unnamable pain
Drew over me out of the merciless miles of the plain,—

Oh, now, unafraid, I am fain to face
  The vast sweet visage of space.
To the edge of the wood I am drawn, I am drawn,
Where the gray beach glimmering runs, as a belt of the dawn,
  For a mete and a mark
    To the forest-dark :—
        So :
Affable live-oak, leaning low,—
Thus—with your favor—soft, with a reverent hand,
(Not lightly touching your person, Lord of the land!)
Bending your beauty aside, with a step I stand
On the firm-packed sand,
        Free
By a world of marsh that borders a world of sea.

Sinuous southward and sinuous northward the shimmering
    band
Of the sand-beach fastens the fringe of the marsh to the
    folds of the land.
Inward and outward to northward and southward the beach-
    lines linger and curl
As a silver-wrought garment that clings to and follows the
    firm sweet limbs of a girl.
Vanishing, swerving, evermore curving again into sight,
Softly the sand-beach wavers away to a dim gray looping of
    light.
And what if behind me to westward the wall of the woods
    stands high?
The world lies east: how ample, the marsh and the sea and
    the sky!
A league and a league of marsh-grass, waist-high, broad in
    the blade,
Green, and all of a height, and unflecked with a light or a
    shade,
Stretch leisurely off, in a pleasant plain,
To the terminal blue of the main.

Oh, what is abroad in the marsh and the terminal sea?
    Somehow my soul seems suddenly free
From the weighing of fate and the sad discussion of sin,
By the length and the breadth and the sweep of the marshes
    of Glynn.

Ye marshes, how candid and simple and nothing-withhold-
    ing and free
Ye publish yourselves to the sky and offer yourselves to the
    sea!

Tolerant plains, that suffer the sea and the rains and the sun,
Ye spread and span like the catholic man who hath mightily
    won
God out of knowledge and good out of infinite pain
And sight out of blindness and purity out of a stain.

As the marsh-hen secretly builds on the watery sod,
Behold I will build me a nest on the greatness of God :
I will fly in the greatness of God as the marsh-hen flies
In the freedom that fills all the space 'twixt the marsh and
    the skies :
By so many roots as the marsh-grass sends in the sod
I will heartily lay me a-hold on the greatness of God :
Oh, like to the greatness of God is the greatness within
The range of the marshes, the liberal marshes of Glynn.

And the sea lends large, as the marsh : lo, out of his plenty
    the sea
Pours fast : full soon the time of the flood-tide must be :
Look how the grace of the sea doth go
About and about through the intricate channels that flow
    Here and there,
        Everywhere,
Till his waters have flooded the uttermost creeks and the
    low-lying lanes,
And the marsh is meshed with a million veins,
That like as with rosy and silvery essences flow
  In the rose-and-silver evening glow.
       Farewell, my lord Sun !
The creeks overflow : a thousand rivulets run
'Twixt the roots of the sod ; the blades of the marsh-grass
    stir ;
Passeth a hurrying sound of wings that westward whirr ;

Passeth, and all is still ; and the currents cease to run ;
And the sea and the marsh are one.

How still the plains of the waters be !
The tide is in his ecstasy.
The tide is at his highest height :
               And it is night.

And now from the Vast of the Lord will the waters of sleep
Roll in on the souls of men,
But who will reveal to our waking ken
The forms that swim and the shapes that creep
              Under the waters of sleep ?
And I would I could know what swimmeth below when the
    tide comes in
On the length and the breadth of the marvellous marshes of
    Glynn.

BALTIMORE, 1878.

CLOVER.

INSCRIBED TO THE MEMORY OF JOHN KEATS.

DEAR uplands, Chester's favorable fields,
My large unjealous Loves, many yet one—
A grave good-morrow to your Graces, all,
Fair tilth and fruitful seasons!
                Lo, how still!
The midmorn empties you of men, save me ;
Speak to your lover, meadows! None can hear.
I lie as lies yon placid Brandywine,
Holding the hills and heavens in my heart
For contemplation.
            'Tis a perfect hour.
From founts of dawn the fluent autumn day
Has rippled as a brook right pleasantly
Half-way to noon ; but now with widening turn
Makes pause, in lucent meditation locked,
And rounds into a silver pool of morn,
Bottom'd with clover-fields. My heart just hears
Eight lingering strokes of some far village-bell,
That speak the hour so inward-voiced, meseems
Time's conscience has but whispered him eight hints
Of revolution. Reigns that mild surcease
That stills the middle of each rural morn—
When nimble noises that with sunrise ran
About the farms have sunk again to rest ;
When Tom no more across the horse-lot calls
To sleepy Dick, nor Dick husk-voiced upbraids
The sway-back'd roan for stamping on his foot
With sulphurous oath and kick in flank, what time
The cart-chain clinks across the slanting shaft,

And, kitchenward, the rattling bucket plumps
Souse down the well, where quivering ducks quack loud,
And Susan Cook is singing.
                              Up the sky
The hesitating moon slow trembles on,
Faint as a new-washed soul but lately up
From out a buried body.   Far about,
A hundred slopes in hundred fantasies
Most ravishingly run, so smooth of curve
That I but seem to see the fluent plain
Rise toward a rain of clover-blooms, as lakes
Pout gentle mounds of plashment up to meet
Big shower-drops.   Now the little winds, as bees,
Bowing the blooms come wandering where I lie
Mixt soul and body with the clover-tufts,
Light on my spirit, give from wing and thigh
Rich pollens and divine sweet irritants
To every nerve, and freshly make report
Of inmost Nature's secret autumn-thought
Unto some soul of sense within my frame
That owns each cognizance of the outlying five,
And sees, hears, tastes, smells, touches, all in one.

Tell me, dear Clover (since my soul is thine,
Since I am fain give study all the day,
To make thy ways my ways, thy service mine,
To seek me out thy God, my God to be,
And die from out myself to live in thee)—
Now, Cousin Clover, tell me in mine ear :
Go'st thou to market with thy pink and green ?
Of what avail, this color and this grace?
Wert thou but squat of stem and brindle-brown,
Still careless herds would feed.   A poet, thou :
What worth, what worth, the whole of all thine art ?
Three-Leaves, instruct me !   I am sick of price.

Framed in the arching of two clover-stems
Where-through I gaze from off my hill, afar,
The spacious fields from me to Heaven take on
Tremors of change and new significance
To th' eye, as to the ear a simple tale
Begins to hint a parable's sense beneath.
The prospect widens, cuts all bounds of blue
Where horizontal limits bend, and spreads
Into a curious-hill'd and curious-valley'd Vast,
Endless before, behind, around ; which seems
Th' incalculable Up and-Down of Time
Made plain before mine eyes.   The clover-stems
Still cover all the space ; but now they bear,
For clover-blooms, fair, stately heads of men
With poets' faces heartsome, dear and pale—
Sweet visages of all the souls of time
Whose loving service to the world has been
In the artist's way expressed and bodied.   Oh,.
In arms' reach, here be Dante, Keats, Chopin,
Raphael, Lucretius, Omar, Angelo,
Beethoven, Chaucer, Schubert, Shakespeare, Bach,
And Buddha (sweetest masters !   Let me lay
These arms this once, this humble once, about
Your reverend necks—the most containing clasp,
For all in all, this world e'er saw !) and there,
Yet further on, bright throngs unnamable
Of workers worshipful, nobilities
In the Court of Gentle Service, silent men,
Dwellers in woods, brooders on helpful art,
And all the press of them, the fair, the large,
That wrought with beauty.
              Lo, what bulk is here ?
Now comes the Course-of-things, shaped like an Ox,
Slow browsing, o'er my hillside, ponderously—-
The huge-brawned, tame, and workful Course-of-things,

That hath his grass, if earth be round or flat,
And hath his grass, if empires plunge in pain
Or faiths flash out.   This cool, unasking Ox
Comes browsing o'er my hills and vales of Time,
And thrusts me out his tongue, and curls it, sharp,
And sicklewise, about my poets' heads,
And twists them in, all—Dante, Keats, Chopin,
Raphael, Lucretius, Omar, Angelo,
Beethoven, Chaucer, Schubert, Shakespeare, Bach,
And Buddha, in one sheaf—and champs and chews,
With slantly-churning jaws, and swallows down ;
Then slowly plants a mighty forefoot out,
And makes advance to futureward, one inch.
So : they have played their part.
                           And to this end ?
This, God ?   This, troublous-breeding Earth ?   This, Sun
Of hot, quick pains ?   To this no-end that ends,
These Masters wrought, and wept, and sweated blood,
And burned, and loved, and ached with public shame,
And found no friends to breathe their loves to, save
Woods and wet pillows ?   This was all ?   This Ox ?
" Nay," quoth a sum of voices in mine ear,
" God's clover, we, and feed His Course of-things ;
The pasture is God's pasture ; systems strange
Of food and fiberment He hath, whereby
The general brawn is built for plans of His
To quality precise.   Kinsman, learn this :
The artist's market is the heart of man ;
The artist's price, some little good of man.
Tease not thy vision with vain search for ends.
The End of Means is art that works by love.
The End of Ends . . . in God's Beginning's lost."

WEST CHESTER, PA., Summer of 1876.

THE WAVING OF THE CORN.

PLOUGHMAN, whose gnarly hand yet kindly wheeled
Thy plough to ring this solitary tree
   With clover, whose round plat, reserved a-field,
In cool green radius twice my length may be—
   Scanting the corn thy furrows else might yield,
To pleasure August, bees, fair thoughts, and me,
      That here come oft together—daily I,
      Stretched prone in summer's mortal ecstasy,
Do stir with thanks to thee, as stirs this morn
      With waving of the corn.

Unseen, the farmer's boy from round the hill
Whistles a snatch that seeks his soul unsought,
   And fills some time with tune, howbeit shrill;
The cricket tells straight on his simple thought—
   Nay, 'tis the cricket's way of being still;
The peddler bee drones in, and gossips naught;
      Far down the wood, a one-desiring dove
      Times me the beating of the heart of love:
And these be all the sounds that mix, each morn,
      With waving of the corn.

From here to where the louder passions dwell,
Green leagues of hilly separation roll:
   Trade ends where yon far clover ridges swell.
Ye terrible Towns, ne'er claim the trembling soul
   That, craftless all to buy or hoard or sell,
From out your deadly complex quarrel stole
      To company with large amiable trees,
      Suck honey summer with unjealous bees,
And take Time's strokes as softly as this morn
      Takes waving of the corn.

WEST CHESTER, PA., 1876.

SONG OF THE CHATTAHOOCHEE.

OUT of the hills of Habersham,
  Down the valleys of Hall,
I hurry amain to reach the plain,
Run the rapid and leap the fall,
Split at the rock and together again,
Accept my bed, or narrow or wide,
And flee from folly on every side
With a lover's pain to attain the plain
    Far from the hills of Habersham,
    Far from the valleys of Hall.

All down the hills of Habersham,
  All through the valleys of Hall,
The rushes cried *Abide, abide,*
The willful waterweeds held me thrall,
The laving laurel turned my tide,
The ferns and the fondling grass said *Stay,*
The dewberry dipped for to work delay,
And the little reeds sighed *Abide, abide,*
    Here in the hills of Habersham,
    Here in the valleys of Hall.

High o'er the hills of Habersham,
  Veiling the valleys of Hall,
The hickory told me manifold
Fair tales of shade, the poplar tall
Wrought me her shadowy self to hold,
The chestnut, the oak, the walnut, the pine,
Overleaning, with flickering meaning and sign,

Said, *Pass not, so cold, these manifold*
   Deep shades of the hills of Habersham,
   These glades in the valleys of Hall.

    And oft in the hills of Habersham,
    And oft in the valleys of Hall,
The white quartz shone, and the smooth brook-stone
Did bar me of passage with friendly brawl,
And many a luminous jewel lone
—Crystals clear or a-cloud with mist,
Ruby, garnet and amethyst—
Made lures with the lights of streaming stone
    In the clefts of the hills of Habersham,
    In the beds of the valleys of Hall.

    But oh, not the hills of Habersham,
    And oh, not the valleys of Hall
Avail : I am fain for to water the plain.
Downward the voices of Duty call—
Downward, to toil and be mixed with the main,
The dry fields burn, and the mills are to turn,
And a myriad flowers mortally yearn,
And the lordly main from beyond the plain
    Calls o'er the hills of Habersham,
    Calls through the valleys of Hall.

1877.

   2

FROM THE FLATS.

WHAT heartache—ne'er a hill!
Inexorable, vapid, vague and chill
The drear sand-levels drain my spirit low.
With one poor word they tell me all they know;
Whereat their stupid tongues, to tease my pain,
Do drawl it o'er again and o'er again.
They hurt my heart with griefs I cannot name:
    Always the same, the same.

    Nature hath no surprise,
No ambuscade of beauty 'gainst mine eyes
From brake or lurking dell or deep defile;
No humors, frolic forms—this mile, that mile;
No rich reserves or happy-valley hopes
Beyond the bend of roads, the distant slopes.
Her fancy fails, her wild is all run tame
    Ever the same, the same.

    Oh might I through these tears
But glimpse some hill my Georgia high uprears,
Where white the quartz and pink the pebble shine,
The hickory heavenward strives, the muscadine
Swings o'er the slope, the oak's far-falling shade
Darkens the dogwood in the bottom glade,
And down the hollow from a ferny nook
Bright leaps a living brook!

TAMPA, FLORIDA, 1877.

THE MOCKING BIRD.

SUPERB and sole, upon a pluméd spray
That o'er the general leafage boldly grew,
He summ'd the woods in song ; or typic drew
The watch of hungry hawks, the lone dismay
Of languid doves when long their lovers stray,
And all birds' passion-plays that sprinkle dew
At morn in brake or bosky avenue.
Whate'er birds did or dreamed, this bird could say.
Then down he shot, bounced airily along
The sward, twitched in a grasshopper, made song
Midflight, perched, prinked, and to his art again.
Sweet Science, this large riddle read me plain :
How may the death of that dull insect be
The life of yon trim Shakspere on the tree ?

TAMPA ROBINS.

THE robin laughed in the orange-tree :
" Ho, windy North, a fig for thee :
While breasts are red and wings are bold
And green trees wave us globes of gold,
   Time's scythe shall reap but bliss for me
   —Sunlight, song, and the orange-tree.

Burn, golden globes in leafy sky,
My orange-planets : crimson I
Will shine and shoot among the spheres
(Blithe meteor that no mortal fears)
   And thrid the heavenly orange-tree
   With orbits bright of minstrelsy.

If that I hate wild winter's spite—
The gibbet trees, the world in white,
The sky but gray wind over a grave—
Why should I ache, the season's slave ?
   I'll sing from the top of the orange-tree
   Gramercy, winter's tyranny.

I 'll south with the sun, and keep my clime ;
My wing is king of the summer-time ;
My breast to the sun his torch shall hold ;
And I 'll call down through the green and gold
   Time, take thy scythe, reap bliss for me,
   Bestir thee under the orange-tree."

TAMPA, FLORIDA, 1877.

THE CRYSTAL.

AT midnight, death's and truth's unlocking time,
When far within the spirit's hearing rolls
The great soft rumble of the course of things—
A bulk of silence in a mask of sound,—
When darkness clears our vision that by day
Is sun-blind, and the soul's a ravening owl
For truth and flitteth here and there about
Low-lying woody tracts of time and oft
Is minded for to sit upon a bough,
Dry-dead and sharp, of some long-stricken tree
And muse in that gaunt place,—'twas then my heart,
Deep in the meditative dark, cried out :

" Ye companies of governor-spirits grave,
  Bards, and old bringers-down of flaming news
  From steep-wall'd heavens, holy malcontents,
  Sweet seers, and stellar visionaries, all
  That brood about the skies of poesy,
  Full bright ye shine, insuperable stars ;
  Yet, if a man look hard upon you, none
  With total lustre blazeth, no, not one
  But hath some heinous freckle of the flesh
  Upon his shining cheek, not one but winks
  His ray, opaqued with intermittent mist
  Of defect ; yea, you masters all must ask
  Some sweet forgiveness, which we leap to give,
  We lovers of you, heavenly-glad to meet
  Your largesse so with love, and interplight
  Your geniuses with our mortalities.

Thus unto thee, O sweetest Shakspere sole,
A hundred hurts a day I do forgive
('Tis little, but, enchantment! 'tis for thee) :
Small curious quibble ; Juliet's prurient pun
In the poor, pale face of Romeo's fancied death ;
Cold rant of Richard ; Henry's fustian roar
Which frights away that sleep he invocates ;
Wronged Valentine's unnatural haste to yield :
Too-silly shifts of maids that mask as men
In faint disguises that could ne'er disguise—
Viola, Julia, Portia, Rosalind ;
Fatigues most drear, and needless overtax
Of speech obscure that had as lief be plain ;
Last I forgive (with more delight, because
'Tis more to do) the labored-lewd discourse
That e'en thy young invention's youngest heir
Besmirched the world with.

                              Father Homer, thee,
Thee also I forgive thy sandy wastes
Of prose and catalogue, thy drear harangues
That tease the patience of the centuries,
Thy sleazy scrap of story,—but a rogue's
Rape of a light-o'-love,—too soiled a patch
To broider with the gods.

                              Thee, Socrates,
Thou dear and very strong one, I forgive
Thy year-worn cloak, thine iron stringencies
That were but dandy upside-down, thy words
Of truth that, mildlier spoke, had mainlier wrought.

So, Buddha, beautiful! I pardon thee
That all the All thou hadst for needy man
Was Nothing, and thy Best of being was
But not to be.

Worn Dante, I forgive
The implacable hates that in thy horrid hells
Or burn or freeze thy fellows, never loosed
By death, nor time, nor love.

And I forgive
Thee, Milton, those thy comic-dreadful wars
Where, armed with gross and inconclusive steel,
Immortals smite immortals mortalwise
And fill all heaven with folly.

Also thee,
Brave Æschylus, thee I forgive, for that
Thine eye, by bare bright justice basilisked,
Turned not, nor ever learned to look where Love
Stands shining.

So, unto thee, Lucretius mine
(For oh, what heart hath loved thee like to this
That's now complaining?), freely I forgive
Thy logic poor, thine error rich, thine earth
Whose graves eat souls and all.

Yea, all you hearts
Of beauty, and sweet righteous lovers large :
Aurelius fine, oft superfine ; mild Saint
A Kempis, overmild ; Epictetus,
Whiles low in thought, still with old slavery tinct ;
Rapt Behmen, rapt too far ; high Swedenborg,
O'ertoppling ; Langley, that with but a touch
Of art hadst sung Piers Plowman to the top
Of English songs, whereof 'tis dearest, now,
And most adorable ; Cædmon, in the morn
A-calling angels with the cow-herd's call
That late brought up the cattle ; Emerson,

Most wise, that yet, in finding Wisdom, lost
Thy Self, sometimes; tense Keats, with angels' nerves
Where men's were better; Tennyson, largest voice
Since Milton, yet some register of wit
Wanting ;—all, all, I pardon, ere 'tis asked,
Your more or less, your little mole that marks
You brother and your kinship seals to man.

But Thee, but Thee, O sovereign Seer of time,
But Thee, O poets' Poet, Wisdom's Tongue,
But Thee, O man's best Man, O love's best Love,
O perfect life in perfect labor writ,
O all men's Comrade, Servant, King, or Priest,—
What *if* or *yet*, what mole, what flaw, what lapse,
What least defect or shadow of defect,
What rumor, tattled by an enemy,
Of inference loose, what lack of grace
Even in torture's grasp, or sleep's, or death's,—
Oh, what amiss may I forgive in Thee,
Jesus, good Paragon, thou Crystal Christ?"

BALTIMORE, 1880.

THE REVENGE OF HAMISH.

It was three slim does and a ten-tined buck in the bracken
    lay;
    And all of a sudden the sinister smell of a man,
    Awaft on a wind-shift, wavered and ran
Down the hill-side and sifted along through the bracken and
    passed that way.

Then Nan got a-tremble at nostril; she was the daintiest
    doe;
    In the print of her velvet flank on the velvet fern
    She reared, and rounded her ears in turn.
Then the buck leapt up, and his head as a king's to a crown
    did go

Full high in the breeze, and he stood as if Death had the
    form of a deer;
    And the two slim does long lazily stretching arose,
    For their day-dream slowlier came to a close,
Till they woke and were still, breath-bound with waiting and
    wonder and fear.

Then Alan the huntsman sprang over the hillock, the hounds
    shot by,
    The does and the ten-tined buck made a marvellous bound,
    The hounds swept after with never a sound,
But Alan loud winded his horn in sign that the quarry was
    nigh.
    2*

For at dawn of that day proud Maclean of Lochbuy to the
    hunt had waxed wild,
    And he cursed at old Alan till Alan fared off with the
      hounds
    For to drive him the deer to the lower glen-grounds :
" I will kill a red deer," quoth Maclean, " in the sight of the
    wife and the child."

So gayly he paced with the wife and the child to his chosen
    stand ;
    But he hurried tall Hamish the henchman ahead : " Go
      turn,'—
Cried Maclean—" if the deer seek to cross to the burn,
Do thou turn them to me : nor fail, lest thy back be red as
    thy hand."

Now hard-fortuned Hamish, half blown of his breath with
    the height of the hill,
    Was white in the face when the ten-tined buck and the does
    Drew leaping to burn-ward ; huskily rose
His shouts, and his nether lip twitched, and his legs were
    o'er-weak for his will.

So the deer darted lightly by Hamish and bounded away to
    the burn.
    But Maclean never bating his watch tarried waiting below.
    Still Hamish hung heavy with fear for to go
All the space of an hour ; then he went, and his face was
    greenish and stern,

And his eye sat back in the socket, and shrunken the eye-
    balls shone,
    As withdrawn from a vision of deeds it were shame to see.

" Now, now, grim henchman, what is 't with thee ? "
Brake Maclean, and his wrath rose red as a beacon the wind
    hath upblown.

" Three does and a ten-tined buck made out," spoke Ham-
    ish, full mild,
  " And I ran for to turn, but my breath it was blown, and
    they passed ;
  I was weak, for ye called ere I broke me my fast."
Cried Maclean : " Now a ten-tined buck in the sight of the
    wife and the child

I had killed if the gluttonous kern had not wrought me a
    snail's own wrong ! "
  Then he sounded, and down came kinsmen and clansmen
    all :
  " Ten blows, for ten tine, on his back let fall,
And reckon no stroke if the blood follow not at the bite of
    thong ! "

So Hamish made bare, and took him his strokes ; at the last
    he smiled.
  " Now I'll to the burn," quoth Maclean, " for it still may
    be,
  If a slimmer-paunched henchman will hurry with me,
I shall kill me the ten-tined buck for a gift to the wife and
    the child ! "

Then the clansmen departed, by this path and that ; and
    over the hill
  Sped Maclean with an outward wrath for an inward
    shame ;

And that place of the lashing full quiet became ;
And the wife and the child stood sad ; and bloody-backed
    Hamish sat still.

But look ! red Hamish has risen ; quick about and about
    turns he.
   " There is none betwixt me and the crag-top ! " he
    screams under breath.
   Then, livid as Lazarus lately from death,
He snatches the child from the mother, and clambers the
    crag toward the sea.

Now the mother drops breath ; she is dumb, and her heart
    goes dead for a space,
   Till the motherhood, mistress of death, shrieks, shrieks
    through the glen,
   And that place of the lashing is live with men,
And Maclean, and the gillie that told him, dash up in a des-
    perate race.

Not a breath's time for asking ; an eye-glance reveals all the
    tale untold.
   They follow mad Hamish afar up the crag toward the sea,
   And the lady cries : " Clansmen, run for a fee !—
Yon castle and lands to the two first hands that shall hook
    him and hold

Fast Hamish back from the brink ! "—and ever she flies up
    the steep,
   And the clansmen pant, and they sweat, and they jostle
    and strain.
   But, mother, 'tis vain ; but, father, 'tis vain ;
Stern Hamish stands bold on the brink, and dangles the
    child o'er the deep.

Now a faintness falls on the men that run, and they all stand
still.
And the wife prays Hamish as if he were God, on her knees,
Crying: "Hamish! O Hamish! but please, but please
For to spare him!" and Hamish still dangles the child, with
a wavering will.

On a sudden he turns; with a sea-hawk scream, and a gibe,
and a song,
Cries: "So; I will spare ye the child if, in sight of ye all,
Ten blows on Maclean's bare back shall fall,
And ye reckon no stroke if the blood follow not at the bite of
the thong!"

Then Maclean he set hardly his tooth to his lip that his tooth
was red,
Breathed short for a space, said : "Nay, but it never shall
be!
Let me hurl off the damnable hound in the sea!"
But the wife : "Can Hamish go fish us the child from the
sea, if dead?

Say yea!—Let them lash *me*, Hamish?"—"Nay!"—"Hus-
band, the lashing will heal;
But, oh, who will heal me the bonny sweet bairn in his
grave?
Could ye cure me my heart with the death of a knave?
Quick! Love! I will bare thee—so—kneel!" Then Mac-
lean 'gan slowly to kneel

With never a word, till presently downward he jerked to the
earth.
Then the henchman—he that smote Hamish—would trem-
ble and lag;

"Strike, hard!" quoth Hamish, full stern, from the crag;
Then he struck him, and "One!" sang Hamish, and danced
    with the child in his mirth.

And no man spake beside Hamish; he counted each stroke
    with a song.
  When the last stroke fell, then he moved him a pace
    down the height,
  And he held forth the child in the heartaching sight
Of the mother, and looked all pitiful grave, as repenting a
    wrong.

And there as the motherly arms stretched out with the thanks-
    giving prayer—
  And there as the mother crept up with a fearful swift pace,
  Till her finger nigh felt of the bairnie's face—
In a flash fierce Hamish turned round and lifted the child in
    the air,

And sprang with the child in his arms from the horrible
    height in the sea,
  Shrill screeching, "Revenge!" in the wind-rush; and
    pallid Maclean,
  Age-feeble with anger and impotent pain,
Crawled up on the crag, and lay flat, and locked hold of dead
    roots of a tree—

And gazed hungrily o'er, and the blood from his back drip-
    dripped in the brine,
  And a sea-hawk flung down a skeleton fish as he flew,
  And the mother stared white on the waste of blue,
And the wind drove a cloud to seaward, and the sun began
    to shine.

Baltimore, 1878.

TO BAYARD TAYLOR.

To range, deep-wrapt, along a heavenly height,
　O'erseeing all that man but undersees;
To loiter down lone alleys of delight,
　And hear the beating of the hearts of trees,
And think the thoughts that lilies speak in white
　By greenwood pools and pleasant passages;

With healthy dreams a-dream in flesh and soul,
　To pace, in mighty meditations drawn,
From out the forest to the open knoll
　Where much thyme is, whence blissful leagues of lawn
Betwixt the fringing woods to southward roll
　By tender inclinations; mad with dawn,

Ablaze with fires that flame in silver dew
　When each small globe doth glass the morning-star,
Long ere the sun, sweet-smitten through and through
　With dappled revelations read afar,
Suffused with saintly ecstasies of blue
　As all the holy eastern heavens are,—

To fare thus fervid to what daily toil
　Employs thy spirit in that larger Land
Where thou art gone; to strive, but not to moil
　In nothings that do mar the artist's hand,
Not drudge unriched, as grain rots back to soil,—
　No profit out of death,—going, yet still at stand,—

Giving what life is here in hand to-day
    For that that's in to-morrow's bush, perchance,—
Of this year's harvest none in the barn to lay,
    All sowed for next year's crop,—a dull advance
In curves that come but by another way
    Back to the start,—a thriftless thrift of ants

Whose winter wastes their summer; O my Friend,
    Freely to range, to muse, to toil, is thine:
Thine, now, to watch with Homer sails that bend
    Unstained by Helen's beauty o'er the brine
Tow'rds some clean Troy no Hector need defend
    Nor flame devour; or, in some mild moon's shine,

Where amiabler winds the whistle heed,
    To sail with Shelley o'er a bluer sea,
And mark Prometheus, from his fetters freed,
    Pass with Deucalion over Italy,
While bursts the flame from out his eager reed
    Wild-stretching towards the West of destiny;

Or, prone with Plato, Shakspere and a throng
    Of bards beneath some plane-tree's cool eclipse
To gaze on glowing meads where, lingering long,
    Psyche's large Butterfly her honey sips;
Or, mingling free in choirs of German song,
    To learn of Goethe's life from Goethe's lips;

These, these are thine, and we, who still are dead,
    Do yearn—nay, not to kill thee back again
Into this charnel life, this lowlihead,

Not to the dark of sense, the blinking brain,
The hugged delusion drear, the hunger fed
  On husks of guess, the monarchy of pain,

The cross of love, the wrench of faith, the shame
  Of science that cannot prove proof is, the twist
Of blame for praise and bitter praise for blame,
  The silly stake and tether round the wrist
By fashion fixed, the virtue that doth claim
  The gains of vice, the lofty mark that's missed

By all the mortal space 'twixt heaven and hell,
  The soul's sad growth o'er stationary friends
Who hear us from our height not well, not well,
  The slant of accident, the sudden bends
Of purpose tempered strong, the gambler's spell,
  The son's disgrace, the plan that e'er depends

On others' plots, the tricks that passion plays
  (I loving you, you him, he none at all),
The artist's pain—to walk his blood-stained ways,
  A special soul, yet judged as general—
The endless grief of art, the sneer that s ays,
  The war, the wound, the groan, the funeral pall—

Not into these, bright spirit, do we yearn
  To bring thee back, but oh, to be, to be
Unbound of all these gyves, to stretch, to spurn
  The dark from off our dolorous lids, to see
Our spark, Conjecture, blaze and sunwise burn,
  And suddenly to stand again by thee !

Ah, not for us, not yet, by thee to stand :
    For us, the fret, the dark, the thorn, the chill ;
For us, to call across unto thy Land,
    " Friend, get thee to the ministrels' holy hill,
And kiss those brethren for us, mouth and hand,
    And make our duty to our master Will."

BALTIMORE, 1879.

A DEDICATION.

TO CHARLOTTE CUSHMAN.

As Love will carve dear names upon a tree,
Symbol of gravure on his heart to be,

So thought I thine with loving text to set
In the growth and substance of my canzonet;

But, writing it, my tears begin to fall—
This wild-rose stem for thy large name's too small!

Nay, still my trembling hands are fain, are fain
Cut the good letters though they lap again;

Perchance such folk as mark the blur and stain
Will say, *It was the beating of the rain;*

Or, haply these o'er-woundings of the stem
May loose some little balm, to plead for them.

1876.

TO CHARLOTTE CUSHMAN.

LOOK where a three-point star shall weave his beam
Into the slumb'rous tissue of some stream,
Till his bright self o'er his bright copy seem
Fulfillment dropping on a come-true dream.;
So in this night of art thy soul doth show
Her excellent double in the steadfast flow
Of wishing love that through men's hearts doth go :
At once thou shin'st above and shin'st below.
E 'en when thou strivest there within Art's sky
(Each star must o'er a strenuous orbit fly),
Full calm thine image in our love doth lie,
A Motion glassed in a Tranquillity.
So triple-rayed, thou mov'st, yet stay'st, serene—
Art's artist, Love's dear woman, Fame's good queen !

BALTIMORE, 1875.

THE STIRRUP-CUP.

DEATH, thou 'rt a cordial old and rare :
Look how compounded, with what care !
Time got his wrinkles reaping thee
Sweet herbs from all antiquity.

David to thy distillage went,
Keats, and Gotama excellent,
Omar Khayyam, and Chaucer bright,
And Shakspere for a king-delight.

Then, Time, let not a drop be spilt :
Hand me the cup whene'er thou wilt ;
'Tis thy rich stirrup-cup to me ;
I'll drink it down right smilingly.

TAMPA, FLORIDA, 1877.

A SONG OF ETERNITY IN TIME.

ONCE, at night, in the manor wood
My Love and I long silent stood,
Amazed that any heavens could
Decree to part us, bitterly repining.
My Love, in aimless love and grief,
Reached forth and drew aside a leaf
That just above us played the thief
And stole our starlight that for us was shining.

A star that had remarked her pain
Shone straightway down that leafy lane,
And wrought his image, mirror-plain,
Within a tear that on her lash hung gleaming.
" Thus Time," I cried, " is but a tear
Some one hath wept 'twixt hope and fear,
Yet in his little lucent sphere
Our star of stars, Eternity, is beaming."

MACON, GEORGIA, 1867.   Revised in 1879.

OWL AGAINST ROBIN.

FROWNING, the owl in the oak complained him
Sore, that the song of the robin restrained him
Wrongly of slumber, rudely of rest.
"From the north, from the east, from the south and the west,
Woodland, wheat-field, corn-field, clover,
Over and over and over and over,
Five o'clock, ten o'clock, twelve, or seven,
Nothing but robin-songs heard under heaven :
       How can we sleep ?

Peep ! you whistle, and *cheep ! cheep ! cheep !*
Oh, peep, if you will, and buy, if 'tis cheap,
And have done; for an owl must sleep.
Are ye singing for fame, and who shall be first?
Each day 's the same, yet the last is worst,
And the summer is cursed with the silly outburst
Of idiot red-breasts peeping and cheeping
By day, when all honest birds ought to be sleeping.
Lord, what a din !   And so out of all reason.
Have ye not heard that each thing hath its season?
Night is to work in, night is for play-time ;
       Good heavens, not day-time !

A vulgar flaunt is the flaring day,
The impudent, hot, unsparing day,
That leaves not a stain nor a secret untold,—
Day the reporter,—the gossip of old,—
Deformity's tease,—man's common scold—

Poh ! Shut the eyes, let the sense go numb
When day down the eastern way has come.
'Tis clear as the moon (by the argument drawn
From Design) that the world should retire at dawn.
Day kills.   The leaf and the laborer breathe
Death in the sun, the cities seethe,
The mortal black marshes bubble with heat
And puff up pestilence ; nothing is sweet
Has to do with the sun : even virtue will taint
(Philosophers say) and manhood grow faint
In the lands where the villainous sun has sway
Through the livelong drag of the dreadful day.
What Eden but noon-light stares it tame,
Shadowless, brazen, forsaken of shame ?
For the sun tells lies on the landscape,—now
Reports me the *what*, unrelieved with the *how*,—
As messengers lie, with the facts alone,
Delivering the word and withholding the tone.

But oh, the sweetness, and oh, the light
Of the high-fastidious night !
Oh, to awake with the wise old stars—
The cultured, the careful, the Chesterfield stars,
That wink at the work-a-day fact of crime
And shine so rich through the ruins of time
That Baalbec is finer than London ; oh,
To sit on the bough that zigzags low
                    By the woodland pool,
And loudly laugh at man, the fool
That vows to the vulgar sun ; oh, rare,
To wheel from the wood to the window where
A day-worn sleeper is dreaming of care,
And perch on the sill and straightly stare
Through his visions ; rare, to sail
Aslant with the hill and a-curve with the vale,—

To flit down the shadow-shot-with-gleam,
Betwixt hanging leaves and starlit stream,
Hither, thither, to and fro,
Silent, aimless, dayless, slow
(*Aimless ? Field-mice ?* True, they're slain,
But the night-philosophy hoots at pain,
Grips, eats quick, and drops the bones
In the water beneath the bough, nor moans
At the death life feeds on).   Robin, pray
      Come away, come away
To the cultus of night.   Abandon the day.
Have more to think and have less to say.
And *cannot* you walk now ? Bah ! don't hop !
      Stop !
Look at the owl, scarce seen, scarce heard,
O irritant, iterant, maddening bird ! "

BALTIMORE, 1880.

3

A SONG OF THE FUTURE.

SAIL fast, sail fast,
Ark of my hopes, Ark of my dreams;
Sweep lordly o'er the drownèd Past,
Fly glittering through the sun's strange beams;
Sail fast, sail fast.
Breaths of new buds from off some drying lea
With news about the Future scent the sea:
My brain is beating like the heart of Haste:
I'll loose me a bird upon this Present waste;
Go, trembling song,
And stay not long; oh, stay not long:
Thou 'rt only a gray and sober dove,
But thine eye is faith and thy wing is love.

BALTIMORE, 1878.

OPPOSITION.

Of fret, of dark, of thorn, of chill,
    Complain no more; for these, O heart,
Direct the random of the will
    As rhymes direct the rage of art.

The lute's fixt fret, that runs athwart
    The strain and purpose of the string,
For governance and nice consort
    Doth bar his wilful wavering.

The dark hath many dear avails;
    The dark distils divinest dews;
The dark is rich with nightingales,
    With dreams, and with the heavenly Muse.

Bleeding with thorns of petty strife,
    I'll ease (as lovers do) my smart
With sonnets to my lady Life
    Writ red in issues from the heart.

What grace may lie within the chill
    Of favor frozen fast in scorn!
When Good's a freeze, we call it Ill!
    This rosy Time is glacier-born.

Of fret, of dark, of thorn, of chill,
    Complain thou not, O heart; for these
Bank-in the current of the will
    To uses, arts, and charities.

BALTIMORE, 1879-80.

ROSE-MORALS.

I.—RED.

WOULD that my songs might be
　　What roses make by day and night—
Distillments of my clod of misery
　　Into delight.

　Soul, could'st thou bare thy breast
　　As yon red rose, and dare the day,
All clean, and large, and calm with velvet rest?
　　Say yea—say yea!

　Ah, dear my Rose, good-bye;
　　The wind is up; so; drift away.
That songs from me as leaves from thee may fly,
　　I strive, I pray.

II.—WHITE.

　Soul, get thee to the heart
　　Of yonder tuberose: hide thee there—
There breathe the meditations of thine art
　　Suffused with prayer.

　Of spirit grave yet light,
　　How fervent fragrances uprise
Pure-born from these most rich and yet most white
　　Virginities!

　Mulched with unsavory death,
　　Grow, Soul! unto such white estate,
That virginal-prayerful art shall be thy breath,
　　Thy work, thy fate.

BALTIMORE, 1875.

CORN.

TO-DAY the woods are trembling through and through
With shimmering forms, that flash before my view,
Then melt in green as dawn-stars melt in blue.
   The leaves that wave against my cheek caress
   Like women's hands; the embracing boughs express
      A subtlety of mighty tenderness;
   The copse-depths into little noises start,
   That sound anon like beatings of a heart,
   Anon like talk 'twixt lips not far apart.
   The beech dreams balm, as a dreamer hums a song;
   Through that vague wafture, expirations strong
   Throb from young hickories breathing deep and long
With stress and urgence bold of prisoned spring
      And ecstasy of burgeoning.
   Now, since the dew-plashed road of morn is dry,
   Forth venture odors of more quality
   And heavenlier giving. Like Jove's locks awry,
      Long muscadines
Rich-wreathe the spacious foreheads of great pines,
And breathe ambrosial passion from their vines.
   I pray with mosses, ferns and flowers shy
   That hide like gentle nuns from human eye
   To lift adoring perfumes to the sky.
I hear faint bridal-sighs of brown and green
Dying to silent hints of kisses keen
As far lights fringe into a pleasant sheen.
   I start at fragmentary whispers, blown
   From undertalks of leafy souls unknown,
   Vague purports sweet, of inarticulate tone.

Dreaming of gods, men, nuns and brides, between
Old companies of oaks that inward lean
To join their radiant amplitudes of green
   I slowly move, with ranging looks that pass
   Up from the matted miracles of grass
Into yon veined complex of space
Where sky and leafage interlace
   So close, the heaven of blue is seen
   Inwoven with a heaven of green.

I wander to the zigzag-cornered fence
Where sassafras, intrenched in brambles dense,
Contests with stolid vehemence
   The march of culture, setting limb and thorn
   As pikes against the army of the corn.

There, while I pause, my fieldward-faring eyes
Take harvests, where the stately corn-ranks rise,
     Of inward dignities
And large benignities and insights wise,
     Graces and modest majesties.
Thus, without theft. I reap another's field ;
Thus, without tilth, I house a wondrous yield,
And heap my heart with quintuple crops concealed.

Look, out of line one tall corn-captain stands
Advanced beyond the foremost of his bands,
   And waves his blades upon the very edge
   And hottest thicket of the battling hedge.
Thou lustrous stalk, that ne'er mayst walk nor talk,
   Still shalt thou type the poet-soul sublime
   That leads the vanward of his timid time
   And sings up cowards with commanding rhyme—

Soul calm, like thee, yet fain, like thee, to grow
By double increment, above, below;
   Soul homely, as thou art, yet rich in grace like thee,
   Teaching the yeomen selfless chivalry
   That moves in gentle curves of courtesy;
Soul filled like thy long veins with sweetness tense,
      By every godlike sense
Transmuted from the four wild elements.
       Drawn to high plans,
   Thou lift'st more stature than a mortal man's,
Yet ever piercest downward in the mould
     And keepest hold
   Upon the reverend and steadfast earth
     That gave thee birth;
   Yea, standest smiling in thy future grave,
     Serene and brave,
   With unremitting breath
   Inhaling life from death,
Thine epitaph writ fair in fruitage eloquent,
     Thyself thy monument.

      As poets should,
Thou hast built up thy hardihood
With universal food,
   Drawn in select proportion fair
   From honest mould and vagabond air;
From darkness of the dreadful night,
     And joyful light;
   From antique ashes, whose departed flame
   In thee has finer life and longer fame;
From wounds and balms,
From storms and calms,
From potsherds and dry bones
    And ruin-stones.

Into thy vigorous substance thou hast wrought
Whate'er the hand of Circumstance hath brought ;
   Yea, into cool solacing green hast spun
   White radiance hot from out the sun.
So thou dost mutually leaven
Strength of earth with grace of heaven ;
   So thou dost marry new and old
   Into a one of higher mould ;
   So thou dost reconcile the hot and cold,
      The dark and bright,
And many a heart-perplexing opposite,
        And so,
   Akin by blood to high and low,
Fitly thou playest out thy poet's part,
Richly expending thy much-bruiséd heart
   In equal care to nourish lord in hall
      Or beast in stall :
   Thou took'st from all that thou mightst give to all.

O steadfast dweller on the selfsame spot
Where thou wast born, that still repinest not—
Type of the home-fond heart, the happy lot !—
   Deeply thy mild content rebukes the land
   Whose flimsy homes, built on the shifting sand
Of trade, for ever rise and fall
With alternation whimsical,
   Enduring scarce a day,
   Then swept away
By swift engulfments of incalculable tides
Whereon capricious Commerce rides.
Look, thou substantial spirit of content !
Across this little vale, thy continent,
   To where, beyond the mouldering mill,
   Yon old deserted Georgian hill

Bares to the sun his piteous aged crest
      And seamy breast,
  By restless-hearted children left to lie
  Untended there beneath the heedless sky,
  As barbarous folk expose their old to die.
Upon that generous-rounding side,
      With gullies scarified
  Where keen Neglect his lash hath plied,
Dwelt one I knew of old, who played at toil,
And gave to coquette Cotton soul and soil.
  Scorning the slow reward of patient grain,
  He sowed his heart with hopes of swifter gain,
  Then sat him down and waited for the rain.
He sailed in borrowed ships of usury—
A foolish Jason on a treacherous sea,
Seeking the Fleece and finding misery.
  Lulled by smooth rippling loans, in idle trance
  He lay, content that unthrift Circumstance
  Should plough for him the stony field of Chance.
Yea, gathering crops whose worth no man might tell,
He staked his life on games of Buy-and-Sell,
And turned each field into a gambler's hell.
    Aye, as each year began,
  My farmer to the neighboring city ran ;
Passed with a mournful anxious face
Into the banker's inner place ;
Parleyed, excused, pleaded for longer grace ;
  Railed at the drought, the worm, the rust, the grass ;
  Protested ne'er again 'twould come to pass ;
  With many an *oh* and *if* and *but alas*
Parried or swallowed searching questions rude,
And kissed the dust to soften Dives's mood.
At last, small loans by pledges great renewed,
  He issues smiling from the fatal door,
  And buys with lavish hand his yearly store
  3*

Till his small borrowings will yield no more.
Aye, as each year declined,
With bitter heart and ever-brooding mind
He mourned his fate unkind.
 In·dust, in rain, with might and main,
 He nursed his cotton, cursed his grain,
 Fretted for news that made him fret again,
Snatched at each telegram of Future Sale,
And thrilled with Bulls' or Bears' alternate wail—
In hope or fear alike for ever pale.
 And thus from year to year, through hope and fear,
 With many a curse and many a secret tear,
 Striving in vain his cloud of debt to clear,
   At last
He woke to find his foolish dreaming past,
 And all his best-of-life the easy prey
 Of squandering scamps and quacks that lined his way
   With vile array,
From rascal statesman down to petty knave ;
Himself, at best, for all his bragging brave,
A gamester's catspaw and a banker's slave.
 Then, worn and gray, and sick with deep unrest,
 He fled away into the oblivious West,
   Unmourned, unblest.

Old hill ! old hill ! thou gashed and hairy Lear
Whom the divine Cordelia of the year,
E'en pitying Spring, will vainly strive to cheer—
 King, that no subject man nor beast may own,
 Discrowned, undaughtered and alone—
Yet shall the great God turn thy fate,
And bring thee back into thy monarch state
  And majesty immaculate.
 Lo, through hot waverings of the August morn,

Thou givest from thy vasty sides forlorn
Visions of golden treasuries of corn—
Ripe largesse lingering for some bolder heart
That manfully shall take thy part,
  And tend thee,
  And defend thee,
With antique sinew and with modern art.

SUNNYSIDE, GEORGIA, August, 1874.

THE SYMPHONY.

" O TRADE ! O Trade ! would thou wert dead !
   The Time needs heart—'tis tired of head :
   We're all for love," the violins said.
" Of what avail the rigorous tale
   Of bill for coin and box for bale ?
   Grant thee, O Trade ! thine uttermost hope :
   Level red gold with blue sky-slope,
   And base it deep as devils grope :
   When all 's done, what hast thou won
   Of the only sweet that 's under the sun ?
   Ay, canst thou buy a single sigh
   Of true love's least, least ecstasy ? "
Then, with a bridegroom's heart-beats trembling,
   All the mightier strings assembling
   Ranged them on the violins' side
   As when the bridegroom leads the bride,
   And, heart in voice, together cried :
" Yea, what avail the endless tale
   Of gain by cunning and plus by sale ?
   Look up the land, look down the land
   The poor, the poor, the poor, they stand
   Wedged by the pressing of Trade's hand
   Against an inward-opening door
   That pressure tightens evermore :
   They sigh a monstrous foul-air sigh
   For the outside leagues of liberty,
   Where Art, sweet lark, translates the sky
   Into a heavenly melody.
' Each day, all day ' (these poor folks say),
' In the same old year-long, drear-long way,

We weave in the mills and heave in the kilns,
We sieve mine-meshes under the hills,
And thieve much gold from the Devil's bank tills,
To relieve, O God, what manner of ills?—
The beasts, they hunger, and eat, and die;
And so do we, and the world's a sty;
Hush, fellow-swine: why nuzzle and cry?
Swinehood hath no remedy
Say many men, and hasten by,
Clamping the nose and blinking the eye.
But who said once, in the lordly tone,
Man shall not live by bread alone
But all that cometh from the Throne?
    Hath God said so?
    But Trade saith *No:*
And the kilns and the curt-tongued mills say *Go:*
There's plenty that can, if you can't: we know.
Move out, if you think you're underpaid.
The poor are prolific; we're not afraid;
    Trade is trade.' "
Thereat this passionate protesting
Meekly changed, and softened till
It sank to sad requesting
And suggesting sadder still:
" And oh, if men might some time see
How piteous-false the poor decree
That trade no more than trade must be!
Does business mean, *Die, you—live, I?*
Then ' Trade is trade' but sings a lie:
'Tis only war grown miserly.
If business is battle, name it so:
War-crimes less will shame it so,
And widows less will blame it so.
Alas, for the poor to have some part
In yon sweet living lands of Art,

Makes problem not for head, but heart.
Vainly might Plato's brain revolve it :
Plainly the heart of a child could solve it."

And then, as when from words that seem but rude
We pass to silent pain that sits abrood
Back in our heart's great dark and solitude,
So sank the strings to gentle throbbing
Of long chords change-marked with sobbing—
Motherly sobbing, not distinctlier heard
Than half wing-openings of the sleeping bird,
Some dream of danger to her young hath stirred.
Then stirring and demurring ceased, and lo !
Every least ripple of the strings' song-flow
Died to a level with each level bow
And made a great chord tranquil-surfaced so,
As a brook beneath his curving bank doth go
To linger in the sacred dark and green
Where many boughs the still pool overlean
And many leaves make shadow with their sheen.
    But presently
A velvet flute-note fell down pleasantly
Upon the bosom of that harmony,
And sailed and sailed incessantly,
As if a petal from a wild-rose blown
Had fluttered down upon that pool of tone
And boatwise dropped o' the convex side
And floated down the glassy tide
And clarified and glorified
The solemn spaces where the shadows bide.
From the warm concave of that fluted note
Somewhat, half song, half odor, forth did float,
As if a rose might somehow be a throat :
" When Nature from her far-off glen
    Flutes her soft messages to men,

The flute can say them o'er again;
Yea, Nature, singing sweet and lone,
Breathes through life's strident polyphone
The flute-voice in the world of tone.
Sweet friends.
Man's love ascends
To finer and diviner ends
Than man's mere thought e'er comprehends.
For I, e'en I,
As here I lie,
A petal on a harmony,
Demand of Science whence and why
Man's tender pain, man's inward cry,
When he doth gaze on earth and sky?
I am not overbold:
I hold
Full powers from Nature manifold.
I speak for each no-tonguéd tree
That, spring by spring, doth nobler be,
And dumbly and most wistfully
His mighty prayerful arms outspreads
Above men's oft-unheeding heads,
And his big blessing downward sheds.
I speak for all-shaped blooms and leaves,
Lichens on stones and moss on eaves,
Grasses and grains in ranks and sheaves;
Broad-fronded ferns and keen-leaved canes,
And briery mazes bounding lanes,
And marsh-plants, thirsty-cupped for rains,
And milky stems and sugary veins;
For every long-armed woman-vine
That round a piteous tree doth twine;
For passionate odors, and divine
Pistils, and petals crystalline;
All purities of shady springs,

All shynesses of film-winged things
That fly from tree-trunks and bark-rings;
All modesties of mountain-fawns
That leap to covert from wild lawns,
And tremble if the day but dawns;
All sparklings of small beady eyes
Of birds, and sidelong glances wise
Wherewith the jay hints tragedies;
All piquancies of prickly burs,
And smoothnesses of downs and furs
Of eiders and of minevers;
All limpid honeys that do lie
At stamen-bases, nor deny
The humming-birds' fine roguery,
Bee-thighs, nor any butterfly;
All gracious curves of slender wings,
Bark-mottlings, fibre-spiralings,
Fern-wavings and leaf-flickerings;
Each dial-marked leaf and flower-bell
Wherewith in every lonesome dell
Time to himself his hours doth tell;
All tree-sounds, rustlings of pine cones,
Wind-sighings, doves' melodious moans,
And night's unearthly under-tones;
All placid lakes and waveless deeps,
All cool reposing mountain-steeps,
Vale-calms and tranquil lotos-sleeps;—
Yea, all fair forms, and sounds, and lights,
And warmths, and mysteries, and mights,
Of Nature's utmost depths and heights,
—These doth my timid tongue present,
Their mouthpiece and leal instrument
And servant, all love-eloquent.
I heard, when '*All for love*' the violins cried:
So, Nature calls through all her system wide,

Give me thy love, O man, so long denied.
Much time is run, and man hath changed his ways,
Since Nature, in the antique fable-days,
Was hid from man's true love by proxy fays,
False fauns and rascal gods that stole her praise.
The nymphs, cold creatures of man's colder brain,
Chilled Nature's streams till man's warm heart was fain
Never to lave its love in them again.
Later, a sweet Voice *Love thy neighbor* said;
Then first the bounds of neighborhood outspread
Beyond all confines of old ethnic dread.
Vainly the Jew might wag his covenant head:
'*All men are neighbors,*' so the sweet Voice said.
So, when man's arms had circled all man's race,
The liberal compass of his warm embrace
Stretched bigger yet in the dark bounds of space;
With hands a-grope he felt smooth Nature's grace,
Drew her to breast and kissed her sweetheart face:
Yea man found neighbors in great hills and trees
And streams and clouds and suns and birds and bees,
And throbbed with neighbor-loves in loving these.
But oh, the poor! the poor! the poor!
That stand by the inward opening door
Trade's hand doth tighten ever more,
And sigh their monstrous foul-air sigh
For the outside hills of liberty,
Where Nature spreads her wild blue sky
For Art to make into melody!
Thou Trade! thou king of the modern days!
    Change thy ways,
    Change thy ways;
Let the sweaty laborers file
    A little while,
    A little while,
Where Art and Nature sing and smile.

Trade ! is thy heart all dead, all dead ?
And hast thou nothing but a head ?
I 'm all for heart," the flute-voice said,
And into sudden silence fled,
Like as a blush that while 'tis red
Dies to a still, still white instead.

Thereto a thrilling calm succeeds,
Till presently the silence breeds
A little breeze among the reeds
That seems to blow by sea-marsh weeds :
Then from the gentle stir and fret
Sings out the melting clarionet,
Like as a lady sings while yet
Her eyes with salty tears are wet.
" O Trade ! O Trade !" the Lady said,
" I too will wish thee utterly dead
If all thy heart is in thy head.
For O my God ! and O my God !
What shameful ways have women trod
At beckoning of Trade's golden rod !
Alas when sighs are traders' lies,
And heart's-ease eyes and violet eyes
        Are merchandise !
O purchased lips that kiss with pain !
O cheeks coin-spotted with smirch and stain !
O trafficked hearts that break in twain !
—And yet what wonder at my sisters' crime ?
So hath Trade withered up Love's sinewy prime,
Men love not women as in olden time.
Ah, not in these cold merchantable days
Deem men their life an opal gray, where plays
The one red Sweet of gracious ladies'-praise.
Now, comes a suitor with sharp prying eye—
Says, *Here, you Lady, if you 'll sell, I 'll buy :*

Come, heart for heart—a trade ?   What ! weeping ? why ?
Shame on such wooers' dapper mercery !
I would my lover kneeling at my feet
In humble manliness should cry, *O sweet !*
I know not if thy heart my heart will greet :
I ask not if thy love my love can meet :
Whate'er thy worshipful soft tongue shall say,
I'll kiss thine answer, be it yea or nay :
I do but know I love thee, and I pray
To be thy knight until my dying day.
Woe him that cunning trades in hearts contrives !
Base love good women to base loving drives.
If men loved larger, larger were our lives ;
And wooed they nobler, won they nobler wives."

There thrust the bold straightforward horn
To battle for that lady lorn,
With heartsome voice of mellow scorn,
Like any knight in knighthood's morn.
  " Now comfort thee," said he,
    " Fair Lady.
For God shall right thy grievous wrong,
And man shall sing thee a true-love song,
Voiced in act his whole life long,
  Yea, all thy sweet life long,
    Fair Lady.
Where's he that craftily hath said,
The day of chivalry is dead ?
I'll prove that lie upon his head,
  Or I will die instead,
    Fair Lady.
Is Honor gone into his grave ?
Hath Faith become a caitiff knave,
And Selfhood turned into a slave
  To work in Mammon's cave,

Fair Lady?
Will Truth's long blade ne'er gleam again?
Hath Giant Trade in dungeons slain
All great contempts of mean-got gain
   And hates of inward stain,
     Fair Lady?
For aye shall name and fame be sold,
And place be hugged for the sake of gold,
And smirch-robed Justice feebly scold
   At Crime all money-bold,
     Fair Lady?
Shall self-wrapt husbands aye forget
Kiss-pardons for the daily fret
Wherewith sweet wifely eyes are wet—
   Blind to lips kiss-wise set—
     Fair Lady?
Shall lovers higgle, heart for heart,
Till wooing grows a trading mart
Where much for little, and all for part,
   Make love a cheapening art,
     Fair Lady?
Shall woman scorch for a single sin
That her betrayer may revel in,
And she be burnt, and he but grin
   When that the flames begin,
     Fair Lady?
Shall ne'er prevail the woman's plea,
We maids would far, far whiter be
If that our eyes might sometimes see
   Men maids in purity,
     Fair Lady?
Shall Trade aye salve his conscience-aches
With jibes at Chivalry's old mistakes—
The wars that o'erhot knighthood makes
   For Christ's and ladies' sakes,

Fair Lady ?
Now by each knight that e'er hath prayed
To fight like a man and love like a maid,
Since Pembroke's life, as Pembroke's blade,
   I' the scabbard, death, was laid,
      Fair Lady,
I dare avouch my faith is bright
That God doth right and God hath might.
Nor time hath changed His hair to white,
   Nor His dear love to spite,
      Fair Lady.
I doubt no doubts : I strive, and shrive my clay,
And fight my fight in the patient modern way
For true love and for thee—ah me ! and pray
   To be thy knight until my dying day,
      Fair Lady."
Made end that knightly horn, and spurred away
Into the thick of the melodious fray.

And then the hautboy played and smiled,
And sang like any large-eyed child,
Cool-hearted and all undefiled.
   " Huge Trade ! " he said,
" Would thou wouldst lift me on thy head
And run where'er my finger led !
Once said a Man—and wise was He—
Never shalt thou the heavens see,
Save as a little child thou be."
Then o'er sea-lashings of commingling tunes
The ancient wise bassoons,
    Like weird
    Gray-beard
Old harpers sitting on the high sea-dunes,
    Chanted runes :

" Bright-waved gain, gray waved loss,
The sea of all doth lash and toss,
One wave forward and one across :
But now 'twas trough, now 'tis crest,
And worst doth foam and flash to best,
        And curst to blest.

Life ! Life ! thou sea-fugue, writ from east to west,
        Love, Love alone can pore
        On thy dissolving score
        Of harsh half-phrasings,
          Blotted ere writ,
        And double erasings
          Of chords most fit.
Yea, Love, sole music master blest,
May read thy weltering palimpsest.
To follow Time's dying melodies through,
And never to lose the old in the new,
And ever to solve the discords true—
        Love alone can do.
And ever Love hears the poor-folks' crying,
And ever Love hears the women's sighing,
And ever sweet knighthood's death-defying,
And ever wise childhood's deep implying,
But never a trader's glozing and lying.

And yet shall Love himself be heard,
Though long deferred, though long deferred :
O'er the modern waste a dove hath whirred :
Music is Love in search of a word."

BALTIMORE, 1875.

MY SPRINGS.

In the heart of the Hills of Life, I know
Two springs that with unbroken flow
Forever pour their lucent streams
Into my soul's far Lake of Dreams.

Not larger than two eyes, they lie
Beneath the many-changing sky
And mirror all of life and time,
—Serene and dainty pantomime.

Shot through with lights of stars and dawns,
And shadowed sweet by ferns and fawns,
—Thus heaven and earth together vie
Their shining depths to sanctify.

Always when the large Form of Love
Is hid by storms that rage above,
I gaze in my two springs and see
Love in his very verity.

Always when Faith with stifling stress
Of grief hath died in bitterness,
I gaze in my two springs and see
A Faith that smiles immortally.

Always when Charity and Hope,
In darkness bounden, feebly grope,
I gaze in my two springs and see
A Light that sets my captives free.

Always, when Art on perverse wing
Flies where I cannot hear him sing,
I gaze in my two springs and see
A charm that brings him back to me.

When Labor faints, and Glory fails,
And coy Reward in sighs exhales,
I gaze in my two springs and see
Attainment full and heavenly.

O Love, O Wife, thine eyes are they,
—My springs from out whose shining gray
Issue the sweet celestial streams
That feed my life's bright Lake of Dreams.

Oval and large and passion-pure
And gray and wise and honor-sure ;
Soft as a dying violet-breath
Yet calmly unafraid of death ;

Thronged, like two dove-cotes of gray doves,
With wife's and mother's and poor-folk's loves,
And home-loves and high glory-loves
And science-loves and story-loves,

And loves for all that God and man
In art and nature make or plan,
And lady-loves for spidery lace
And broideries and supple grace

And diamonds and the whole sweet round
Of littles that large life compound,
And loves for God and God's bare truth,
And loves for Magdalen and Ruth,

Dear eyes, dear eyes and rare complete—
Being heavenly-sweet and earthly-sweet,
—I marvel that God made you mine,
For when He frowns, 'tis then ye shine!

BALTIMORE, 1874.
4

IN ABSENCE.

I.

THE storm that snapped our fate's one ship in twain
   Hath blown my half o' the wreck from thine apart
O Love! O Love! across the gray-waved main
   To thee-ward strain my eyes, my arms, my heart.
I ask my God if e'en in His sweet place,
   Where, by one waving of a wistful wing,
My soul could straightway tremble face to face
   With thee, with thee, across the stellar ring—
Yea, where thine absence I could ne'er bewail
   Longer than lasts that little blank of bliss
When lips draw back, with recent pressure pale,
   To round and redden for another kiss—
      Would not my lonesome heart still sigh for thee
      What time the drear kiss intervals must be?

II.

So do the mottled formulas of Sense
   Glide snakewise through our dreams of Aftertime;
So errors breed in reeds and grasses dense
   That bank our singing rivulets of rhyme.
By Sense rule Space and Time; but in God's Land
   Their intervals are not, save such as lie
Betwixt successive tones in concords bland
   Whose loving distance makes the harmony.

Ah, there shall never come 'twixt me and thee
  Gross dissonances of the mile, the year ;
But in the multichords of ecstasy
  Our souls shall mingle, yet be featured clear,
    And absence, wrought to intervals divine,
    Shall part, yet link, thy nature's tone and mine.

III.

Look down the shining peaks of all my days
  Base-hidden in the valleys of deep night,
So shalt thou see the heights and depths of praise
  My love would render unto love's delight ;
For I would make each day an Alp sublime
  Of passionate snow, white-hot yet icy-clear,
—One crystal of the true-loves of all time
  Spiring the world's prismatic atmosphere ;
And I would make each night an awful vale
  Deep as thy soul, obscure as modesty,
With every star in heaven trembling pale
  O'er sweet profounds where only Love can see.
    Oh, runs not thus the lesson thou hast taught ?—
    When life 's all love, 'tis life : aught else, 'tis naught.

IV.

Let no man say, *He at his lady's feet*
  Lays worship that to Heaven alone belongs ;
Yea, swings the incense that for God is meet
  In flippant censers of light lover's songs.
Who says it, knows not God, nor love, nor thee ;
  For love is large as is yon heavenly dome :
In love's great blue, each passion is full free
  To fly his favorite flight and build his home.

Did e'er a lark with skyward-pointing beak
  Stab by mischance a level-flying dove ?
Wife-love flies level, his dear mate to seek :
  God-love darts straight into the skies above.
      Crossing, the windage of each other's wings
      But speeds them both upon their journeyings.

BALTIMORE, 1874.

ACKNOWLEDGMENT.

I.

O AGE that half believ'st thou half believ'st,
  Half doubt'st the substance of thine own half doubt,
And, half perceiving that thou half perceiv'st,
  Stand'st at thy temple door, heart in, head out!
Lo! while thy heart's within, helping the choir,
  Without, thine eyes range up and down the time,
Blinking at o'er-bright science, smit with desire
  To see and not to see.   Hence, crime on crime.
Yea, if the Christ (called thine) now paced yon street,
  Thy halfness hot with His rebuke would swell;
Legions of scribes would rise and run and beat
  His fair intolerable Wholeness twice to hell.
    Nay (so, dear Heart, thou whisperest in my soul),
    '*T is a half time, yet Time will make it whole.*

II.

Now at thy soft recalling voice I rise
  Where thought is lord o'er Time's complete estate,
Like as a dove from out the gray sedge flies
  To tree-tops green where cooes his heavenly mate.
From these clear coverts high and cool I see
  How every time with every time is knit,
And each to all is mortised cunningly,
  And none is sole or whole, yet all are fit.
Thus, if this Age but as a comma show

'Twixt weightier clauses of large-worded years,
    My calmer soul scorns not the mark : I know
  This crooked point Time's complex sentence clears.
        Yet more I learn while, Friend! I sit by thee :
        Who sees all time, sees all eternity.

III.

If I do ask, How God can dumbness keep
    While Sin creeps grinning through His house of Time,
  Stabbing His saintliest children in their sleep,
    And staining holy walls with clots of crime ?—
  Or, How may He whose wish but names a fact
    Refuse what miser's-scanting of supply
  Would richly glut each void where man hath lacked
    Of grace or bread ?—or, How may Power deny
  Wholeness to th' almost-folk that hurt our hope—
    These heart-break Hamlets who so barely fail
  In life or art that but a hair's more scope
    Had set them fair on heights they ne'er may scale ?—
        Somehow by thee, dear Love, I win content :
        Thy Perfect stops th' Imperfect's argument.

IV.

By the more height of thy sweet stature grown,
    Twice-eyed with thy gray vision set in mine,
  I ken far lands to wifeless men unknown,
    I compass stars for one-sexed eyes too fine.
  No text on sea-horizons cloudily writ,
    No maxim vaguely starred in fields or skies,
  But this wise thou-in-me deciphers it :
    Oh, thou 'rt the Height of heights, the Eye of eyes.

Not hardest Fortune's most unbounded stress
  Can blind my soul nor hurl it from on high,
Possessing thee, the self of loftiness,
  And very light that Light discovers by.
    Howe'er thou turn'st, wrong Earth ! still Love's in sight :
    For we are taller than the breadth of night.

BALTIMORE, 1874-5.

LAUS MARIÆ.

ACROSS the brook of Time man leaping goes
  On stepping-stones of epochs, that uprise
Fixed, memorable, midst broad shallow flows
  Of neutrals, kill-times, sleeps, indifferencies.
So mixt each morn and night rise salient heaps :
  Some cross with but a zigzag, jaded pace
From meal to meal : some with convulsive leaps
  Shake the green tussocks of malign disgrace :
And some advance by system and deep art
  O'er vantages of wealth, place, learning, tact.
But thou within thyself, dear manifold heart,
  Dost bind all epochs in one dainty Fact.
    Oh, sweet, my pretty sum of history,
    I leapt the breadth of Time in loving thee !

BALTIMORE, 1874-5.

SPECIAL PLEADING.

TIME, hurry my Love to me :
Haste, haste ! Lov'st not good company ?
 Here's but a heart-break sandy waste
 'Twixt Now and Then.   Why, killing haste
Were best, dear Time, for thee, for thee !

Oh, would that I might divine
Thy name beyond the zodiac sign
 Wherefrom our times-to-come descend.
 He called thee *Sometime.*   Change it, friend :
Now-time sounds so much more fine !

Sweet Sometime, fly fast to me :
Poor Now time sits in the Lonesome-tree
 And broods as gray as any dove,
 And calls, *When wilt thou come, O Love ?*
And pleads across the waste to thee.

Good Moment, that giv'st him me,
Wast ever in love ?   Maybe, maybe
 Thou 'lt be this heavenly velvet time
 When Day and Night as rhyme and rhyme
Set lip to lip dusk-modestly ;

Or haply some noon afar,
—O life's top bud, mixt rose and star,
 How ever can thine utmost sweet
 Be star-consummate, rose-complete,
Till thy rich reds full opened are ?
 4*

Well, be it dusk-time or noon-time,
I ask but one small boon, Time :
  Come thou in night, come thou in day,
   I care not, I care not : have thine own way,
But only, but only, come soon, Time.

BALTIMORE, 1875.

THE BEE.

WHAT time I paced, at pleasant morn,
   A deep and dewy wood,
I heard a mellow hunting-horn
   Make dim report of Dian's lustihood
Far down a heavenly hollow.
Mine ear, though fain, had pain to follow :
   Tara! it twanged, *tara-tara !* it blew,
   Yet wavered oft, and flew
Most ficklewise about, or here, or there,
A music now from earth and now from air.
      But on a sudden, lo !
      I marked a blossom shiver to and fro
With dainty inward storm ; and there within
A down-drawn trump of yellow jessamine
            A bee
      Thrust up its sad-gold body lustily,
All in a honey madness hotly bound
            On blissful burglary.
            A cunning sound
In that wing-music held me : down I lay
In amber shades of many a golden spray,
Where looping low with languid arms the Vine
In wreaths of ravishment did overtwine
Her kneeling Live-Oak, thousand-fold to plight
Herself unto her own true stalwart knight.

As some dim blur of distant music nears
The long-desiring sense, and slowly clears

To forms of time and apprehensive tune,
 So, as I lay, full soon
Interpretation throve : the bee's fanfare,
Through sequent films of discourse vague as air,
Passed to plain words, while, fanning faint perfume,
The bee o'erhung a rich, unrifled bloom :
 " O Earth, fair lordly Blossom, soft a-shine
 Upon the star-pranked universal vine,
   Hast nought for me ?
    To thee
 Come I, a poet, hereward haply blown,
 From out another worldflower lately flown.
Wilt ask, *What profit e'er a poet brings ?*
He beareth starry stuff about his wings
To pollen thee and sting thee fertile : nay,
If still thou narrow thy contracted way,
  —Worldflower, if thou refuse me—
  —Worldflower, if thou abuse me,
 And hoist thy stamen's spear-point high
 To wound my wing and mar mine eye—
Nathless I 'll drive me to thy deepest sweet,
Yea, richlier shall that pain the pollen beat
From me to thee, for oft these pollens be
Fine dust from wars that poets wage for thee.
But, O beloved Earthbloom soft a-shine
Upon the universal Jessamine,
  Prithee, abuse me not,
  Prithee, refuse me not,
Yield, yield the heartsome honey love to me
  Hid in thy nectary ! "
And as I sank into a dimmer dream
The pleading bee's song-burthen sole did seem :
 " Hast ne'er a honey-drop of love for me
  In thy huge nectary ? "

TAMPA, FLORIDA, 1877.

THE HARLEQUIN OF DREAMS.

SWIFT, through some trap mine eyes have never found,
  Dim-panelled in the painted scene of Sleep,
  Thou, giant Harlequin of Dreams, dost leap
Upon my spirit's stage. Then Sight and Sound,
Then Space and Time, then Language, Mete and Bound,
  And all familiar Forms that firmly keep
  Man's reason in the road, change faces, peep
Betwixt the legs and mock the daily round.
Yet thou canst more than mock : sometimes my tears
  At midnight break through bounden lids—a sign
  Thou hast a heart : and oft thy little leaven
Of dream-taught wisdom works me bettered years.
  In one night witch, saint, trickster, fool divine,
    I think thou 'rt Jester at the Court of Heaven !

BALTIMORE, 1878.

STREET-CRIES.

Oft seems the Time a market-town
　Where many merchant-spirits meet
Who up and down and up and down
　Cry out along the street

Their needs, as wares ; one *thus*, one *so :*
　Till all the ways are full of sound :
—But still come rain, and sun, and snow,
　And still the world goes round.

I.

REMONSTRANCE.

" Opinion, let me alone : I am not thine.
Prim Creed, with categoric point, forbear
　To feature me my Lord by rule and line.
Thou canst not measure Mistress Nature's hair,
　Not one sweet inch : nay, if thy sight is sharp,
Would'st count the strings upon an angel's harp ?
　　Forbear, forbear.

　"Oh let me love my Lord more fathom deep
Than there is line to sound with : let me love
　My fellow not as men that mandates keep :
Yea, all that 's lovable, below, above,
　　That let me love by heart, by heart, because
　　(Free from the penal pressure of the laws)
　　　I find it fair.

" The tears I weep by day and bitter night,
Opinion ! for thy sole salt vintage fall.
　—As morn by morn I rise with fresh delight,
Time through my casement cheerily doth call
　　' Nature is new,' 'tis birthday every day,
　　　Come feast with me, let no man say me nay,
　　　　Whate'er befall.'

" So fare I forth to feast : I sit beside
Some brother bright : but, ere good-morrow's passed,
　Burly Opinion wedging in hath cried
' Thou shalt not sit by us, to break thy fast,
　　Save to our Rubric thou subscribe and swear—
　　Religion hath blue eyes and yellow hair :
　　　She's Saxon, all.'

" Then, hard a-hungered for my brother's grace
Till well-nigh fain to swear his folly's true,
　In sad dissent I turn my longing face
To him that sits on the left : ' Brother,—with you?'
　　—' Nay, not with me, save thou subscribe and swear
　　Religion hath black eyes and raven hair :
　　　Nought else is true.'

" Debarred of banquets that my heart could make
With every man on every day of life,
　I homeward turn, my fires of pain to slake
In deep endearments of a worshipped wife.
　　' I love thee well, dear Love,' quoth she, ' and yet
　　Would that thy creed with mine completely met,
　　　As one, not two.'

" Assassin ! Thief ! Opinion, 'tis thy work.
By Church, by throne, by hearth, by every good
　That's in the Town of Time, I see thee lurk,
And e'er some shadow stays where thou hast stood.

Thou hand'st sweet Socrates his hemlock sour ;
Thou sav'st Barabbas in that hideous hour,
    And stabb'st the good

" Deliverer Christ ; thou rack'st the souls of men ;
Thou tossest girls to lions and boys to flames ;
  Thou hew'st Crusader down by Saracen ;
Thou buildest closets full of secret shames ;
    Indifferent cruel, thou dost blow the blaze
    Round Ridley or Servetus ; all thy days
      Smell scorched ; I would

"—Thou base-born Accident of time and place—
Bigot Pretender unto Judgment's throne—
  Bastard, that claimest with a cunning face
Those rights the true, true Son of Man doth own
    By Love's authority—thou Rebel cold
    At head of civil wars and quarrels old—
      Thou Knife on a throne—

" I would thou left'st me free, to live with love,
And faith, that through the love of love doth find
  My Lord's dear presence in the stars above,
The clods below, the flesh without, the mind
    Within, the bread, the tear, the smile.
    Opinion, damned Intriguer, gray with guile,
      Let me alone."

BALTIMORE, 1878-9.

II.

THE SHIP OF EARTH.

" THOU Ship of Earth, with Death, and Birth, and Life, and
    Sex aboard,
    And fires of Desires burning hotly in the hold,
  I fear thee, O! I fear thee, for I hear the tongue and sword
    At battle on the deck, and the wild mutineers are bold!

" The dewdrop morn may fall from off the petal of the sky,
    But all the deck is wet with blood and stains the crystal
    red.
  A pilot, GOD, a pilot! for the helm is left awry,
    And the best sailors in the ship lie there among the
    dead!"

PRATTVILLE, ALABAMA, 1868.

III.

HOW LOVE LOOKED FOR HELL.

" To heal his heart of long-time pain
  One day Prince Love for to travel was fain
    With Ministers Mind and Sense.
 ' Now what to thee most strange may be ?'
  Quoth Mind and Sense.   ' All things above,
  One curious thing I first would see—
    Hell,' quoth Love.

" Then Mind rode in and Sense rode out:
  They searched the ways of man about.
    First frightfully groaneth Sense.

'''Tis here, 'tis here,' and spurreth in fear
    To the top of the hill that hangeth above
    And plucketh the Prince : '.Come, come, 'tis here—'
        ' Where ? ' quoth Love—

" ' Not far, not far,' said shivering Sense
    As they rode on.   ' A short way hence,
        —But seventy paces hence :
    Look, King, dost see where suddenly
    This road doth dip from the height above ?
    Cold blew a mouldy wind by me '
        (' Cold ? ' quoth Love)

" ' As I rode down, and the River was black,
    And yon-side, lo ! an endless wrack
        And rabble of souls,' sighed Sense,
    ' Their eyes upturned and begged and burned
    In brimstone lakes, and a Hand above
    Beat back the hands that upward yearned—'
        ' Nay ! ' quoth Love—

" ' Yea, yea, sweet Prince ; thyself shalt see,
    Wilt thou but down this slope with me ;
        'Tis palpable,' whispered Sense.
    —At the foot of the hill a living rill
    Shone, and the lilies shone white above ;
    ' But now 'twas black, 'twas a river, this rill,'
        (' Black ? ' quoth Love)

" ' Ay, black, but lo ! the lilies grow,
    And yon-side where was woe, was woe,
        —Where the rabble of souls,' cried Sense,
    ' Did shrivel and turn and beg and burn,
    Thrust back in the brimstone from above—
    Is banked of violet, rose, and fern :'
        ' How ? ' quoth Love :

" 'For lakes of pain, yon pleasant plain
  Of woods and grass and yellow grain
        Doth ravish the soul and sense :
  And never a sigh beneath the sky,
  And folk that smile and gaze above—'
'But saw'st thou here, with thine own eye,
        Hell ? ' quoth Love.

" ' I saw true hell with mine own eye,
    True hell, or light hath told a lie,
        True, verily,' quoth stout Sense.
  Then Love rode round and searched the ground,
  The caves below, the hills above ;
'But I cannot find where thou hast found
        Hell,' quoth Love.

" ' There, while they stood in a green wood
  And marvelled still on Ill and Good,
        Came suddenly Minister Mind.
'In the heart of sin doth hell begin :
  'Tis not below, 'tis not above,
  It lieth within, it lieth within : '
        (' Where ? ' quoth Love)

" 'I saw a man sit by a corse ;
    Hell 's in the murderer's breast : remorse !
        Thus clamored his mind to his mind :
  Not fleshly dole is the sinner's goal,
  Hell 's not below, nor yet above,
  'Tis fixed in the ever-damnèd soul—'
        ' Fixed ? ' quoth Love—

" ' Fixed : follow me, would'st thou but see :
  He weepeth under yon willow tree,
        Fast chained to his corse,' quoth Mind.

Full soon they passed, for they rode fast,
Where the piteous willow bent above.
' Now shall I see at last, at last,
          Hell,' quoth Love.

" There when they came Mind suffered shame :
' These be the same and not the same,'
          A-wondering whispered Mind.
Lo, face by face two spirits pace
Where the blissful willow waves above :
One saith : ' Do me a friendly grace—'
          ('Grace!' quoth Love)

" ' Read me two Dreams that linger long.
Dim as returns of old-time song
          That flicker about the mind.
I dreamed (how deep in mortal sleep !)
I struck thee dead, then stood above,
With tears that none but dreamers weep ; '
          ' Dreams,' quoth Love ;

" ' In dreams, again, I plucked a flower
That clung with pain and stung with power,
          Yea, nettled me, body and mind.'
' 'Twas the nettle of sin, 'twas medicine ;
No need nor seed of it here Above ;
In dreams of hate true loves begin.'
          ' True,' quoth Love.

" ' Now strange,' quoth Sense, and ' Strange,' quoth Mind,
' We saw it, and yet 'tis hard to find,
          —But we saw it,' quoth Sense and Mind.
Stretched on the ground, beautiful-crowned
Of the piteous willow that wreathed above,
But I cannot find where ye have found
          Hell,' quoth Love."

BALTIMORE, 1878-9.

IV.

TYRANNY.

" SPRING-GERMS, spring-germs,
I charge you by your life, go back to death.
This glebe is sick, this wind is foul of breath.
        Stay : feed the worms.

" Oh ! every clod
Is faint, and falters from the war of growth
And crumbles in a dreary dust of sloth,
        Unploughed, untrod

" What need, what need,
To hide with flowers the curse upon the hills,
Or sanctify the banks of sluggish rills
        Where vapors breed ?

" And—if needs must—
Advance, O Summer-heats ! upon the land,
And bake the bloody mould to shards and sand
        And dust.

" Before your birth,
Burn up, O Roses ! with your dainty flame.
Good Violets, sweet Violets, hide shame
        Below the earth.

" Ye silent Mills,
Reject the bitter kindness of the moss.
O Farms ! protest if any tree emboss
        The barren hills.

" Young Trade is dead,
And swart Work sullen sits in the hillside fern
And folds his arms that find no bread to earn,
    And bows his head.

" Spring-germs, spring-germs,
Albeit the towns have left you place to play,
I charge you, sport not.   Winter owns to-day,
    Stay : feed the worms."

PRATTVILLE, ALABAMA, 1868.

V.

LIFE AND SONG.

" IF life were caught by a clarionet,
    And a wild heart, throbbing in the reed,
Should thrill its joy and trill its fret,
    And utter its heart in every deed,

"Then would this breathing clarionet
    Type what the poet fain would be ;
For none o' the singers ever yet
    Has wholly lived his minstrelsy,

" Or clearly sung his true, true thought,
    Or utterly bodied forth his life,
Or out of life and song has wrought
    The perfect one of man and wife ;

' Or lived and sung, that Life and Song
    Might each express the other's all,
Careless if life or art were long
    Since both were one, to stand or fall :

" So that the wonder struck the crowd,
Who shouted it about the land :
His song was only living aloud,
His work, a singing with his hand ! "

1868.

VI.

TO RICHARD WAGNER.

" I SAW a sky of stars that rolled in grime.
All glory twinkled through some sweat of fight,
From each tall chimney of the roaring time
That shot his fire far up the sooty night
Mixt fuels—Labor's Right and Labor's Crime—
Sent upward throb on throb of scarlet light
Till huge hot blushes in the heavens blent
With golden hues of Trade's high firmament.

" Fierce burned the furnaces ; yet all seemed well,
Hope dreamed rich music in the rattling mills.
' Ye foundries, ye shall cast my church a bell,'
Loud cried the Future from the farthest hills :
' Ye groaning forces, crack me every shell
Of customs, old constraints, and narrow ills ;
Thou, lithe Invention, wake and pry and guess,
Till thy deft mind invents me Happiness.'

" And I beheld high scaffoldings of creeds
Crumbling from round Religion's perfect Fane :
And a vast noise of rights, wrongs, powers, needs,
—Cries of new Faiths that called ' This Way is plain,'
—Grindings of upper against lower greeds—
—Fond sighs for old things, shouts for new,—did reign
Below that stream of golden fire that broke,
Mottled with red, above the seas of smoke.

" Hark !   Gay fanfares from halls of old Romance
    Strike through the clouds of clamor : who be these
That, paired in rich processional, advance
    From darkness o'er the murk mad factories
Into yon flaming road, and sink, strange Ministrants !
    Sheer down to earth, with many minstrelsies
And motions fine, and mix about the scene
    And fill the Time with forms of ancient mien ?

" Bright ladies and brave knights of Fatherland ;
    Sad mariners, no harbor e'er may hold,
A swan soft floating tow'rds a magic strand ;
    Dim ghosts, of earth, air, water, fire, steel, gold,
Wind, grief, and love ; a lewd and lurking band
    Of Powers—dark Conspiracy, Cunning cold,
Gray Sorcery ; magic cloaks and rings and rods ;
    Valkyries, heroes, Rhinemaids, giants, gods !
        *   *   *   *   *   *   *   *
" O Wagner, westward bring thy heavenly art,
    No trifler thou : Siegfried and Wotan be
Names for big ballads of the modern heart.
    Thine ears hear deeper than thine eyes can see.
Voice of the monstrous mill, the shouting mart,
    Not less of airy cloud and wave and tree,
Thou, thou, if even to thyself unknown,
    Hast power to say the Time in terms of tone."

1877.

VII.

A SONG OF LOVE.

" HEY, rose, just born
    Twin to a thorn ;
Was 't so with you, O Love and Scorn ?

  " Sweet eyes that smiled,
    Now wet and wild ;
O Eye and Tear—mother and child.

  " Well : Love and Pain
    Be kinsfolk twain :
Yet would, Oh would I could love again."
  5

TO BEETHOVEN.

In o'er-strict calyx lingering,
  Lay music's bud too long unblown,
Till thou, Beethoven, breathed the spring :
  Then bloomed the perfect rose of tone.

O Psalmist of the weak, the strong,
  O Troubadour of love and strife,
Co-Litanist of right and wrong,
  Sole Hymner of the whole of life,

I know not how, I care not why,—
  Thy music sets my world at ease,
And melts my passion's mortal cry
  In satisfying symphonies.

It soothes my accusations sour
  'Gainst thoughts that fray the restless soul :
The stain of death ; the pain of power ;
  The lack of love 'twixt part and whole ;

The yea-nay of Freewill and Fate,
  Whereof both cannot be, yet are ;
The praise a poet wins too late
  Who starves from earth into a star ;

The lies that serve great parties well,
  While truths but give their Christ a cross;
The loves that send warm souls to hell,
  While cold-blood neuters take no loss ;

Th' indifferent smile that nature's grace
   On Jesus, Judas, pours alike ;
Th' indifferent frown on nature's face
   When luminous lightnings strangely strike

The sailor praying on his knees
   And spare his mate that's cursing God ;
How babes and widows starve and freeze,
   Yet Nature will not stir a clod ;

Why Nature blinds us in each act
   Yet makes no law in mercy bend,
No pitfall from our feet retract,
   No storm cry out *Take shelter, friend ;*

Why snakes that crawl the earth should ply
   Rattles, that whoso hears may shun,
While serpent lightnings in the sky,
   But rattle when the deed is done ;

How truth can e'er be good for them
   That have not eyes to bear its strength,
And yet how stern our lights condemn
   Delays that lend the darkness length ;

To know all things, save knowingness ;
   To grasp, yet loosen, feeling's rein ;
To waste no manhood on success ;
   To look with pleasure upon pain ;

Though teased by small mixt social claims,
   To lose no large simplicity,
And midst of clear-seen crimes and shames
   To move with manly purity ;

To hold, with keen, yet loving eyes,
　　Art's realm from Cleverness apart,
To know the Clever good and wise,
　　Yet haunt the lonesome heights of Art ;

O Psalmist of the weak, the strong,
　　O Troubadour of love and strife,
Co-Litanist of right and wrong,
　　Sole Hymner of the whole of life,

I know not how, I care not why,
　　Thy music brings this broil at ease,
And melts my passion's mortal cry
　　In satisfying symphonies.

Yea, it forgives me all my sins,
　　Fits life to love like rhyme to rhyme,
And tunes the task each day begins
　　By the last trumpet-note of Time.

1876-7.

An Frau Nannette Falk=Auerbach.

Als du im Saal mit deiner himmlischen Kunst
    Beethoven zeigst, und seinem Willen nach
Mit den zehn Fingern führst der Leute Gunst,
    Zehn Zungen sagen was der Meister sprach.
Schauend dich an, ich seh', daß nicht allein
    Du sitzest: jetzt herab die Töne ziehn
Beethovens Geist: er steht bei dir, ganz rein:
    Für dich mit Vaters Stolz sein' Augen glühn:
Er sagt, „Ich hörte dich aus Himmelsluft,
    Die kommt ja näher, wo ein Künstler spielt:
Mein Kind (ich sagte) mich zur Erde ruft:
    Ja, weil mein Arm kein Kind im Leben hielt,
Gott hat mir dich nach meinem Tod gegeben,
    Nannette, Tochter! dich, mein zweites Leben!"

Baltimore, 1878.

TO NANNETTE FALK-AUERBACH.

OFT as I hear thee, wrapt in heavenly art,
  The massive message of Beethoven tell
With thy ten fingers to the people's heart
  As if ten tongues told news of heaven and hell,—
Gazing on thee, I mark that not alone,
  Ah, not alone, thou sittest : there, by thee,
Beethoven's self, dear living lord of tone,
  Doth stand and smile upon thy mastery.
Full fain and fatherly his great eyes glow :
  He says, " From Heaven, my child, I heard thee call
(For, where an artist plays, the sky is low):
  Yea, since my lonesome life did lack love's all,
    In death, God gives me thee : thus, quit of pain,
    Daughter, Nannette! in thee I live again."

BALTIMORE, 1878.

TO OUR MOCKING-BIRD.

DIED OF A CAT, MAY, 1878.

I.

TRILLETS of humor,—shrewdest whistle-wit,—
  Contralto cadences of grave desire
  Such as from off the passionate Indian pyre
Drift down through sandal-odored flames that split
About the slim young widow who doth sit
  And sing above,—midnights of tone entire,—
  Tissues of moonlight shot with songs of fire ;—
Bright drops of tune, from oceans infinite
Of melody, sipped off the thin-edged wave
And trickling down the beak,—discourses brave
  Of serious matter that no man may guess,—
  Good-fellow greetings, cries of light distress—
    All these but now within the house we heard :
    O Death, wast thou too deaf to hear the bird ?

II.

Ah me, though never an ear for song, thou hast
  A tireless tooth for songsters : thus of late
  Thou camest, Death, thou Cat ! and leap'st my gate,
And, long ere Love could follow, thou hadst passed
Within and snatched away, how fast, how fast,
  My bird—wit, songs, and all—thy richest freight
  Since that fell time when in some wink of fate
Thy yellow claws unsheathed and stretched, and cast

Sharp hold on Keats, and dragged him slow away,
And harried him with hope and horrid play—
   Ay, him, the world's best wood-bird, wise with song—
   Till thou hadst wrought thine own last mortal wrong.
      'Twas wrong! 'twas wrong! I care not, *wrong's* the word—
      To munch our Keats and crunch our mocking-bird.

III.

Nay, Bird; my grief gainsays the Lord's best right.
   The Lord was fain, at some late festal time,
   That Keats should set all Heaven's woods in rhyme,
And thou in bird-notes. Lo, this tearful night,
Methinks I see thee, fresh from death's despite,
   Perched in a palm-grove, wild with pantomime,
   O'er blissful companies couched in shady thyme,
—Methinks I hear thy silver whistlings bright
Mix with the mighty discourse of the wise,
   Till broad Beethoven, deaf no more, and Keats,
'Midst of much talk, uplift their smiling eyes,
   And mark the music of thy wood-conceits,
      And halfway pause on some large, courteous word,
      And call thee "Brother," O thou heavenly Bird!

BALTIMORE, 1878.

THE DOVE.

IF haply thou, O Desdemona Morn,
  Shouldst call along the curving sphere, "Remain,
Dear Night, sweet Moor ; nay, leave me not in scorn !"
  With soft halloos of heavenly love and pain ;—

Shouldst thou, O Spring ! a-cower in coverts dark,
  'Gainst proud supplanting Summer sing thy plea,
And move the mighty woods through mailèd bark
  Till mortal heart-break throbbed in every tree ;—

Or (grievous *if* that may be *yea* o'er-soon !),
  If thou, my Heart, long holden from thy Sweet,
Shouldst knock Death's door with mellow shocks of tune,
  Sad inquiry to make—*When may we meet?*

Nay, if ye three, O Morn ! O Spring ! O Heart !
  Should chant grave unisons of grief and love ;
Ye could not mourn with more melodious art
  Than daily doth yon dim sequestered dove.

CHADD'S FORD, PENNSYLVANIA, 1877.

5*

TO ——, WITH A ROSE.

I ASKED my heart to say
Some word whose worth my love's devoir might pay
Upon my Lady's natal day.

Then said my heart to me :
*Learn from the rhyme that now shall come to thee
What fits thy Love most lovingly.*

This gift that learning shows ;
For, as a rhyme unto its rhyme-twin goes,
I send a rose unto a Rose.

PHILADELPHIA, 1876.

ON HUNTINGDON'S "MIRANDA."

THE storm hath blown thee a lover, sweet,
And laid him kneeling at thy feet.
But,—guerdon rich for favor rare !
The wind hath all thy holy hair
To kiss and to sing through and to flare
Like torch-flames in the passionate air,
    About thee, O Miranda.

Eyes in a blaze, eyes in a daze,
Bold with love, cold with amaze,
Chaste-thrilling eyes, fast-filling eyes
With daintiest tears of love's surprise,
Ye draw my soul unto your blue
As warm skies draw the exhaling dew,
    Divine eyes of Miranda.

And if I were yon stolid stone,
Thy tender arm doth lean upon,
Thy touch would turn me to a heart,
And I would palpitate and start,
—Content, when thou wert gone, to be
A dumb rock by the lonesome sea
    Forever, O Miranda.

BALTIMORE, 1874.

ODE TO THE JOHNS HOPKINS UNIVERSITY.

READ ON THE FOURTH COMMEMORATION DAY, FEBRUARY, 1880.

How tall among her sisters, and how fair,—
How grave beyond her youth, yet debonair
As dawn, 'mid wrinkled *Matres* of old lands
Our youngest *Alma Mater* modest stands !
In four brief cycles round the punctual sun
Has she, old Learning's latest daughter, won
This grace, this stature, and this fruitful fame.
　　Howbeit she was born
　　Unnoised as any stealing summer morn.
From far the sages saw, from far they came
And ministered to her,
Led by the soaring-genius'd Sylvester
That, earlier, loosed the knot great Newton tied,
And flung the door of Fame's locked temple wide.
As favorable fairies thronged of old and blessed
The cradled princess with their several best,
　　　　So, gifts and dowers meet
　　　　To lay at Wisdom's feet,
These liberal masters largely brought—
Dear diamonds of their long-compressèd thought,
Rich stones from out the labyrinthine cave
Of research, pearls from Time's profoundest wave

And many a jewel brave, of brilliant ray,
   Dug in the far obscure Cathay
      Of meditation deep—
With flowers, of such as keep
Their fragrant tissues and their heavenly hues
Fresh-bathed forever in eternal dews—
   The violet with her low-drooped eye,
   For learnèd modesty,—
The student snow-drop, that doth hang and pore
Upon the earth, like Science, evermore,
And underneath the clod doth grope and grope,—
   The astronomer heliotrope,
That watches heaven with a constant eye,—
The daring crocus, unafraid to try
(When Nature calls) the February snows,—
   And patience' perfect rose.
Thus sped with helps of love and toil and thought,
Thus forwarded of faith, with hope thus fraught,
In four brief cycles round the stringent sun
This youngest sister hath her stature won.

     Nay, why regard
The passing of the years ?   Nor made, nor marr'd,
By help or hindrance of slow Time was she :
O'er this fair growth Time had no mastery :
So quick she bloomed, she seemed to bloom at birth,
As Eve from Adam, or as he from earth.
Superb o'er slow increase of day on day,
Complete as Pallas she began her way ;
Yet not from Jove's unwrinkled forehead sprung,
But long-time dreamed, and out of trouble wrung,
Fore-seen, wise-plann'd, pure child of thought and pain,
Leapt our Minerva from a mortal brain.

And here, O finer Pallas, long remain,—
Sit on these Maryland hills, and fix thy reign,

And frame a fairer Athens than of yore
    In these blest bounds of Baltimore,—
    Here, where the climates meet
That each may make the other's lack complete,—
Where Florida's soft Favonian airs beguile
The nipping North,—where nature's powers smile,—
Where Chesapeake holds frankly forth her hands
Spread wide with invitation to all lands,—
Where now the eager people yearn to find
The organizing hand that fast may bind
Loose straws of aimless aspiration fain
    In sheaves of serviceable grain,—
    Here, old and new in one,
Through nobler cycles round a richer sun
    O'er-rule our modern ways,
O blest Minerva of these larger days!
Call here thy congress of the great, the wise,
The hearing ears, the seeing eyes,—
Enrich us out of every farthest clime,—
Yea, make all ages native to our time,
    Till thou the freedom of the city grant
    To each most antique habitant
      Of Fame,—
Bring Shakspere back, a man and not a name,—
Let every player that shall mimic us
In audience see old godlike Æschylus,—
Bring Homer, Dante, Plato, Socrates,—
Bring Virgil from the visionary seas
Of old romance,—bring Milton, no more blind,—
Bring large Lucretius, with unmaniac mind,—
Bring all gold hearts and high resolvèd wills
To be with us about these happy hills,—
    Bring old Renown
To walk familiar citizen of the town,—

Bring Tolerance, that can kiss and disagree,—
Bring Virtue, Honor, Truth, and Loyalty,—
Bring Faith that sees with undissembling eyes,—
Bring all large Loves and heavenly Charities,—
Till man seem less a riddle unto man
And fair Utopia less Utopian,
And many peoples call from shore to shore,
The world has bloomed again, at Baltimore!

BALTIMORE, 1880.

TO DR. THOMAS SHEARER.

PRESENTING A PORTRAIT-BUST OF THE AUTHOR.

SINCE you, rare friend ! have tied my living tongue
  With thanks more large than man e'er said or sung,
So let the dumbness of this image be
  My eloquence, and still interpret me.

BALTIMORE, 1880.

MARTHA WASHINGTON.

WRITTEN FOR THE "MARTHA WASHINGTON COURT
JOURNAL."

DOWN cold snow-stretches of our bitter time,
  When windy shams and the rain-mocking sleet
Of Trade have cased us in such icy rime
  That hearts are scarcely hot enough to beat,
Thy fame, O Lady of the lofty eyes,
  Doth fall along the age, like as a lane
Of Spring, in whose most generous boundaries
  Full many a frozen virtue warms again.
To-day I saw the pale much-burdened form
  Of Charity come limping o'er the line,
And straighten from the bending of the storm
  And flush with stirrings of new strength divine,
Such influence and sweet gracious impulse came
Out of the beams of thine immortal name !

BALTIMORE, February 22d, 1875.

PSALM OF THE WEST.

LAND of the willful gospel, thou worst and thou best ;
Tall Adam of lands, new-made of the dust of the West ;
Thou wroughtest alone in the Garden of God, unblest
Till He fashioned lithe Freedom to lie for thine Eve on thy
    breast—
    Till out of thy heart's dear neighborhood, out of thy side,
    He fashioned an intimate Sweet one and brought thee a
        Bride.
    Cry hail ! nor bewail that the wound of her coming was
        wide.
Lo, Freedom reached forth where the world as an apple
    hung red ;
Let us taste the whole radiant round of it, gayly she said :
If we die, at the worst we shall lie as the first of the dead.
    Knowledge of Good and of Ill, O Land ! she hath given
        thee ;
    Perilous godhoods of choosing have rent thee and riven
        thee ;
    Will's high adoring to Ill's low exploring hath driven thee—
    Freedom, thy Wife, hath uplifted thy life and clean
        shriven thee !
Her shalt thou clasp for a balm to the scars of thy breast,
Her shalt thou kiss for a calm to thy wars of unrest,
Her shalt extol in the psalm of the soul of the West.
    For Weakness, in freedom, grows stronger than Strength
        with a chain ;
    And Error, in freedom, will come to lamenting his stain,
    Till freely repenting he whiten his spirit again ;

And Friendship, in freedom, will blot out the bounding of
    race ;
And straight Law, in freedom, will curve to the rounding of
    grace ;
And Fashion, in freedom, will die of the lie in her face ;
  And Desire flame white on the sense as a fire on a height,
  And Sex flame white in the soul as a star in the night,
  And Marriage plight sense unto soul as the two-colored
    light
Of the fire and the star shines one with a duplicate might ;
And Science be known as the sense making love to the All,
And Art be known as the soul making love to the All,
And Love be known as the marriage of man with the All—
  Till Science to knowing the Highest shall lovingly turn,
  Till Art to loving the Highest shall consciously burn,
  Till Science to Art as a man to a woman shall yearn,
        —Then morn !
When Faith from the wedding of Knowing and Loving shall
    purely be born,
And the Child shall smile in the West, and the West to the
    East give morn,
And the Time in that ultimate Prime shall forget old regret-
    ting and scorn,
Yea, the stream of the light shall give off in a shimmer the
    dream of the night forlorn.

      Once on a time a soul
      Too full of his dole
In a querulous dream went crying from pole to pole—
  Went sobbing and crying
  For ever a sorrowful song of living and dying,
  How *life was the dropping and death the drying*
  Of a Tear that fell in a day when God was sighing.
And ever Time tossed him bitterly to and fro
As a shuttle inlaying a perilous warp of woe

In the woof of things from terminal snow to snow,
Till, lo !
Rest.
And he sank on the grass of the earth as a lark on its nest,
And he lay in the midst of the way from the east to the west.
Then the East came out from the east and the West from
the west,
And, behold ! in the gravid deeps of the lower dark,
While, above, the wind was fanning the dawn as a spark,
The East and the West took form as the wings of a lark.
One wing was feathered with facts of the uttermost Past,
And one with the dreams of a prophet; and both sailed
fast
And met where the sorrowful Soul on the earth was cast.
Then a Voice said : *Thine, if thou lovest enough to use ;*
But another : *To fly and to sing is pain : refuse !*
Then the Soul said : *Come, O my wings ! I cannot but
choose.*
And the Soul was a-tremble like as a new-born thing,
Till the spark of the dawn wrought a conscience in heart as
in wing,
Saying, *Thou art the lark of the dawn ; it is time to sing.*

Then that artist began in a lark's low circling to pass ;
And first he sang at the height of the top of the grass
A song of the herds that are born and die in the mass.
And next he sang a celestial-passionate round
At the height of the lips of a woman above the ground,
How *Love was a fair true Lady, and Death a wild hound,
And she called, and he licked her hand and with girdle
was bound.*
And then with a universe-love he was hot in the wings,
And the sun stretched beams to the worlds as the shining
strings
Of the large hid harp that sounds when an all-lover sings ;

And the sky's blue traction prevailed o'er the earth's in
    might,
And the passion of flight grew mad with the glory of
    height
And the uttering of song was like to the giving of light ;
And he learned that hearing and seeing wrought nothing
    alone,
And that music on earth much light upon Heaven had
    thrown,
And he melted-in silvery sunshine with silvery tone ;
    And the spirals of music e'er higher and higher he wound
    Till the luminous cinctures of melody up from the ground
    Arose as the shaft of a tapering tower of sound—
    Arose for an unstricken full-finished Babel of sound.
But God was not angry, nor ever confused his tongue,
For not out of selfish nor impudent travail was wrung
The song of all men and all things that the all-lover sung.
    Then he paused at the top of his tower of song on high,
    And the voice of the God of the artist from far in the
    sky
Said, *Son, look down : I will cause that a Time gone by*
Shall pass, and reveal his heart to thy loving eye.

       Far spread, below,
The sea that fast hath locked in his loose flow
All secrets of Atlantis' drownèd woe
    Lay bound about with night on every hand,
    Save down the eastern brink a shining band
    Of day made out a little way from land.
Then from that shore the wind upbore a cry :
Thou Sea, thou Sea of Darkness ! why, oh why
Dost waste thy West in unthrift mystery ?
    But ever the idiot sea-mouths foam and fill,
    And never a wave doth good for man or ill,
    And Blank is king, and Nothing hath his will ;

And like as grim-beaked pelicans level file
Across the sunset toward their nightly isle
On solemn wings that wave but seldomwhile,
   So leanly sails the day behind the day
   To where the Past's lone Rock o'erglooms the spray,
   And down its mortal fissures sinks away.

     Master, Master, break this ban :
       The wave lacks Thee.
     Oh, is it not to widen man
       Stretches the sea?
     Oh, must the sea-bird's idle van
       Alone be free ?

     Into the Sea of the Dark doth creep
       Björne's pallid sail,
     As the face of a walker in his sleep,
       Set rigid and most pale,
     About the night doth peer and peep
       In a dream of an ancient tale.

     Lo, here is made a hasty cry :
       Land, land, upon the west !—
     God save such land !   Go by, go by :
       Here may no mortal rest,
     Where this waste hell of slate doth lie
       And grind the glacier's breast.

     The sail goeth limp : hey, flap and strain !
       Round eastward slanteth the mast ;
     As the sleep-walker waked with pain,
       White-clothed in the midnight blast,
     Doth stare and quake, and stride again
       To houseward all aghast.

Yet as, *A ghost!* his household cry :
He hath followed a ghost in flight.
Let us see the ghost—his household fly
    With lamps to search the night—
So Norsemen's sails run out and try
    The Sea of the Dark with light.

Stout Are Marson, southward whirled
    From out the tempest's hand,
Doth skip the sloping of the world
    To Huitramannaland,
Where Georgia's oaks with moss-beards curled
    Wave by the shining strand,

And sway in sighs from Florida's Spring
    Or Carolina's Palm—
What time the mocking-bird doth bring
    The woods his artist's-balm,
Singing the Song of Everything
    Consummate-sweet and calm—

Land of large merciful-hearted skies,
    Big bounties, rich increase,
Green rests for Trade's blood-shotten eyes,
    For o'er-beat brains surcease,
For Love the dear woods' sympathies,
    For Grief the wise woods' peace,

For Need rich givings of hid powers
    In hills and vales quick-won,
For Greed large exemplary flowers
    That ne'er have toiled nor spun,
For Heat fair-tempered winds and showers,
    For Cold the neighbor sun.

Land where the Spirits of June-Heat
  From out their forest-maze
Stray forth at eve with loitering feet,
  And fervent hymns upraise
In bland accord and passion sweet
  Along the Southern ways :—

" O Darkness, tawny Twin whose Twin hath ceased,
  Thou Odor from the day-flower's crushing born,
Thou visible Sigh out of the mournful East,
  That cannot see her lord again till morn :
O Leaves, with hollow palms uplifted high
  To catch the stars' most sacred rain of light :
O pallid Lily-petals fain to die
  Soul-stung by subtle passion of the night :
O short-breath'd Winds beneath the gracious moon
  Running mild errands for mild violets,
Or carrying sighs from the red lips of June
  What wavering way the odor-current sets :
O Stars wreathed vinewise round yon heavenly dells,
  Or thrust from out the sky in curving sprays,
Or whorled, or looped with pendent flower-bells,
  Or bramble-tangled in a brilliant maze,
Or lying like young lilies in a lake
  About the great white Lily of the moon,
Or drifting white from where in heaven shake
  Star-portraitures of apple trees in June,
Or lapp'd as leaves of a great rose of stars,
  Or shyly clambering up cloud-lattices,
Or trampled pale in the red path of Mars,
  Or trim-set quaint in gardeners'-fantasies :
O long June Night-sounds crooned among the leaves ;
  O whispered confidence of Dark and Green ;
O murmurs in old moss about old eaves ;
  O tinklings floating over water-sheen."

Then Leif, bold son of Eric the Red,
    To the South of the West doth flee—
Past slaty Helluland is sped,
    Past Markland's woody lea,
Till round about fair Vinland's head,
    Where Taunton helps the sea,

The Norseman calls, the anchor falls,
    The mariners hurry a-strand :
They wassail with fore-drunken skals
    Where prophet wild grapes stand ;
They lift the Leifsbooth's hasty walls
    They stride about the land—

New England, thee ! whose ne'er-spent wine
    As blood doth stretch each vein,
And urge thee, sinewed like thy vine,
    Through peril and all pain
To grasp Endeavor's towering Pine,
    And, once ahold, remain—

Land where the strenuous-handed Wind
    With sarcasm of a friend
Doth smite the man would lag behind
    To frontward of his end ;
Yea, where the taunting fall and grind
    Of Nature's Ill doth send

Such mortal challenge of a clown
    Rude-thrust upon the soul,
That men but smile where mountains frown
    Or scowling waters roll,
And Nature's front of battle down
    Do hurl from pole to pole.
    6

Now long the Sea of Darkness glimmers low
With sails from Northland flickering to and fro—
Thorwald, Karlsefne, and those twin heirs of woe,
   Hellboge and Finnge, in treasonable bed
   Slain by the ill-born child of Eric Red,
   Freydisa false.   Till, as much time is fled,
Once more the vacant airs with darkness fill,
Once more the wave doth never good nor ill,
And Blank is king, and Nothing works his will ;
   And leanly sails the day behind the day
   To where the Past's lone Rock o'erglooms the spray,
   And down its mortal fissures sinks away,
As when the grim-beaked pelicans level file
Across the sunset to their seaward isle
On solemn wings that wave but seldomwhile.

       Master, Master, poets sing ;
         The Time calls Thee ;
       Yon Sea binds hard on everything
         Man longs to be :
       Oh, shall the sea-bird's aimless wing
         Alone move free ?

Santa Maria, well thou tremblest down the wave,
   Thy *Pinta* far abow, thy *Niña* nigh astern :
Columbus stands in the night alone, and, passing grave,
   Yearns o'er the sea as tones o'er under-silence yearn.
Heartens his heart as friend befriends his friend less brave,
   Makes burn the faiths that cool, and cools the doubts that
     burn :—

I.

" 'Twixt this and dawn, three hours my soul will smite
   With prickly seconds, or less tolerably
   With dull-blade minutes flatwise slapping me.

Wait, Heart! Time moves.—Thou lithe young Western
    Night,
Just-crownèd king, slow riding to thy right,
    Would God that I might straddle mutiny
    Calm as thou sitt'st yon never-managed sea,
Balk'st with his balking, fliest with his flight,
Giv'st supple to his rearings and his falls,
    Nor dropp'st one coronal star about thy brow
        Whilst ever dayward thou art steadfast drawn!
Yea, would I rode these mad contentious brawls
    No damage taking from their If and How,
        Nor no result save galloping to my Dawn!

II.

" My Dawn? my Dawn?   How if it never break?
    How if this West by other Wests is piecèd,
    And these by vacant Wests on Wests increàsed—
One Pain of Space, with hollow ache on ache
Throbbing and ceasing not for Christ's own sake?—
    Big perilous theorem, hard for king and priest:
        Pursue the West but long enough, 'tis East!
Oh, if this watery world no turning take!
    Oh, if for all my logic, all my dreams,
    Provings of that which is by that which seems,
Fears, hopes, chills, heats, hastes, patiences, droughts,
    tears,
Wife-grievings, slights on love, embezzled years,
    Hates, treaties, scorns, upliftings, loss and gain,—
    This earth, no sphere, be all one sickening plane!

III.

" Or, haply, how if this contrarious West,
    That me by turns hath starved, by turns hath fed,
    Embraced, disgraced, beat back, solicited,
Have no fixed heart of Law within his breast,

Or with some different rhythm doth e'er contest
   Nature in the East ?   Why, 'tis but three weeks fled
   I saw my Judas needle shake his head
And flout the Pole that, east, he Lord confessed !
   God ! if this West should own some other Pole,
   And with his tangled ways perplex my soul
Until the maze grow mortal, and I die
   Where distraught Nature clean hath gone astray,
   On earth some other wit than Time's at play,
Some other God than mine above the sky !

IV.

" Now speaks mine other heart with cheerier seeming :
   Ho, Admiral ! o'er-defalking to thy crew
   Against thyself, thyself far overfew
To front yon multitudes of rebel scheming ?
Come, ye wild twenty years of heavenly dreaming !
   Come, ye wild weeks since first this canvas drew
   Out of vexed Palos ere the dawn was blue,
O'er milky waves about the bows full-creaming !
Come set me round with many faithful spears
   Of confident remembrance—how I crushed
   Cat-lived rebellions, pitfalled treasons, hushed
Scared husbands' heart-break cries on distant wives,
Made cowards blush at whining for their lives,
Watered my parching souls, and dried their tears.

V.

" Ere we Gomera cleared, a coward cried,
   Turn, turn : here be three caravels ahead,
   From Portugal, to take us : we are dead !
Hold Westward, pilot, calmly I replied.

So when the last land down the horizon died,
　　Go back, go back! they prayed : *our hearts are lead.—*
　　Friends, we are bound into the West, I said.
Then passed the wreck of a mast upon our side.
See (so they wept) *God's Warning! Admiral, turn!—*
　　Steersman, I said, *hold straight into the West.*
Then down the night we saw the meteor burn.
　　So do the very heavens in fire protest :
　　Good Admiral, put about ! O Spain, dear Spain !—
　　Hold straight into the West, I said again.

VI.

" Next drive we o'er the slimy-weeded sea.
　　Lo ! herebeneath (another coward cries)
　　The cursèd land of sunk Atlantis lies :
This slime will suck us down—turn while thou'rt free !—
But no ! I said, *Freedom bears West for me !*
　　Yet when the long-time stagnant winds arise,
　　And day by day the keel to westward flies,
My Good my people's Ill doth come to be :
　　Ever the winds into the West do blow ;
　　Never a ship, once turned, might homeward go ;
Meanwhile we speed into the lonesome main.
　　For Christ's sake, parley, Admiral! Turn, before
We sail outside all bounds of help from pain !—
　　Our help is in the West, I said once more.

VII.

" So when there came a mighty cry of *Land !*
　　And we clomb up and saw, and shouted strong
　　Salve Regina ! all the ropes along,
But knew at morn how that a counterfeit band
Of level clouds had aped a silver strand ;

So when we heard the orchard-bird's small song,
And all the people cried, *A hellish throng*
To tempt us onward by the Devil planned,
Yea, all from hell—keen heron, fresh green weeds,
Pelican, tunny-fish, fair tapering reeds,
   Lie-telling lands that ever shine and die
   In clouds of nothing round the empty sky.
Tired Admiral, get thee from this hell, and rest!—
Steersman, I said, *hold straight into the West.*

VIII.

"I marvel how mine eye, ranging the Night,
   From its big circling ever absently
   Returns, thou large low Star, to fix on thee.
Maria! Star? No star: a Light, a Light!
Wouldst leap ashore, Heart? Yonder burns—a Light.
   Pedro Gutierrez, wake! come up to me.
   I prithee stand and gaze about the sea:
What seest? *Admiral, like as land—a Light!*
Well! Sanchez of Segovia, come and try:
What seest? *Admiral, naught but sea and sky!*
   Well! But *I* saw It. Wait! the Pinta's gun!
   Why, look, 'tis dawn, the land is clear: 'tis done!
Two dawns do break at once from Time's full hand—
God's, East—mine, West: good friends, behold my
   Land!"

        Master, Master! faster fly
        Now the hurrying seasons by;
        Now the Sea of Darkness wide
        Rolls in light from side to side;
        Mark, slow drifting to the West
        Down the trough and up the crest,
        Yonder piteous heartsease petal
        Many-motioned rise and settle—

Petal cast a-sea from land
By the awkward-fingered Hand
That, mistaking Nature's course,
Tears the love it fain would force—
Petal calm of heartsease flower
Smiling sweet on tempest sour,
Smiling where by crest and trough
Heartache Winds at heartsease scoff,
Breathing mild perfumes of prayer
'Twixt the scolding sea and air.

Mayflower, piteous Heartsease Petal!
Suavely down the sea-troughs settle,
Gravely breathe perfumes of prayer
'Twixt the scolding sea and air,
Bravely up the sea-hills rise—
Sea-hills slant thee toward the skies.
Master, hold disaster off
From the crest and from the trough;
Heartsease, on the heartache sea
God, thy God, will pilot thee.

Mayflower, Ship of Faith's best Hope!
Thou art sure if all men grope;
Mayflower, Ship of Hope's best Faith!
All is true the great God saith;
Mayflower, Ship of Charity!
Love is Lord of land and sea.
Oh, with love and love's best care
Thy large godly freightage bear—
Godly Hearts that, Grails of gold,
Still the blood of Faith do hold.

Now bold Massachusetts clear
Cuts the rounding of the sphere.

Out the anchor, sail no more,
Lay us by the Future's shore—
Not the shore we sought, 'tis true,
But the time is come to do.
Leap, dear Standish, leap and wade ;
Bradford, Hopkins, Tilley, wade :
Leap and wade ashore and kneel—
God be praised that steered the keel !
Home is good and soft is rest,
Even in this jagged West :
Freedom lives, and Right shall stand ;
Blood of Faith is in the land.

Then in what time the primal icy years
Scraped slowly o'er the Puritans' hopes and fears,
Like as great glaciers built of frozen tears,
    The Voice from far within the secret sky
    Said, *Blood of Faith ye have ?   So ; let us try.*
        And presently
The anxious-masted ships that westward fare,
Cargo'd with trouble and a-list with care,
Their outraged decks hot back to England bear,
Then come again with stowage of worse weight,
Battle, and tyrannous Tax, and Wrong, and Hate,
And all bad items of Death's perilous freight.

O'er Cambridge set the yeomen's mark :
Climb, patriot, through the April dark.
O lanthorn ! kindle fast thy light,
Thou budding star in the April night,
For never a star more news hath told,
Or later flame in heaven shall hold.
Ay, lanthorn on the North Church tower,
When that thy church hath had her hour,

Still from the top of Reverence high
Shalt thou illume Fame's ampler sky ;
For, statured large o'er town and tree,
Time's tallest Figure stands by thee,
And, dim as now thy wick may shine
The Future lights his lamp at thine.

Now haste thee while the way is clear,
      Paul Revere !
Haste, Dawes ! but haste thou not, O Sun !
      To Lexington.

Then Devens looked and saw the light :
He got him forth into the night,
And watched alone on the river-shore,
And marked the British ferrying o'er.

John Parker ! rub thine eyes and yawn :
But one o'clock and yet 'tis Dawn !
Quick, rub thine eyes and draw thy hose :
The Morning comes ere darkness goes.
Have forth and call the yeomen out,
For somewhere, somewhere close about
Full soon a Thing must come to be
Thine honest eyes shall stare to see—
Full soon before thy patriot eyes
Freedom from out of a Wound shall rise.

Then haste ye, Prescott and Revere !
Bring all the men of Lincoln here ;
Let Chelmsford, Littleton, Carlisle,
Let Acton, Bedford, hither file—
Oh hither file, and plainly see
Out of a wound leap Liberty.
    6*

Say, Woodman April! all in green,
Say, Robin April! hast thou seen
In all thy travel round the earth
Ever a morn of calmer birth?
But Morning's eye alone serene
Can gaze across yon village-green
To where the trooping British run
   Through Lexington.

Good men in fustian, stand ye still;
The men in red come o'er the hill.
Lay down your arms, damned Rebels! cry
The men in red full haughtily.
But never a grounding gun is heard;
The men in fustian stand unstirred;
Dead calm, save maybe a wise bluebird
Puts in his little heavenly word.
O men in red! if ye but knew
The half as much as bluebirds do,
Now in this little tender calm
Each hand would out, and every palm
With patriot palm strike brotherhood's stroke
Or ere these lines of battle broke.

O men in red! if ye but knew
The least of the all that bluebirds do,
Now in this little godly calm
Yon voice might sing the Future's Psalm—
The Psalm of Love with the brotherly eyes
Who pardons and is very wise—
Yon voice that shouts, high-hoarse with ire,
   Fire!
The red-coats fire, the homespuns fall:
The homespuns' anxious voices call,

Brother, art hurt? and *Where hit, John?*
And, *Wipe this blood,* and *Men, come on,*
And, *Neighbor, do but lift my head,*
And *Who is wounded? Who is dead?*
Seven are killed. My God! my God!
Seven lie dead on the village sod.
Two Harringtons, Parker, Hadley, Brown,
Monroe and Porter,—these are down.
Nay, look! Stout Harrington not yet dead!
He crooks his elbow, lifts his head.
He lies at the step of his own house-door ;
He crawls and makes a path of gore.
The wife from the window hath seen, and rushed ;
He hath reached the step, but the blood hath gushed ;
He hath crawled to the step of his own house-door,
But his head hath dropped : he will crawl no more.
Clasp, Wife, and kiss, and lift the head :
Harrington lies at his doorstep dead.

But, O ye Six that round him lay
And bloodied up that April day !
As Harrington fell, ye likewise fell—
At the door of the House wherein ye dwell ;
As Harrington came, ye likewise came
And died at the door of your House of Fame.

Go by, old Field of Freedom's hopes and fears ;
Go by, old Field of Brothers' hate and tears :
Behold ! yon home of Brothers' Love appears
    Set in the burnished silver of July,
    On Schuylkill wrought as in old broidery
    Clasped hands upon a shining baldric lie,
New Hampshire, Georgia, and the mighty ten
That lie between, have heard the huge-nibbed pen
Of Jefferson tell the rights of man to men.

They sit in the reverend Hall : *Shall we declare ?*
Floats round about the anxious-quivering air
'Twixt narrow Schuylkill and broad Delaware.
Already, Land! thou *hast* declared : 'tis done.
Ran ever clearer speech than that did run
When the sweet Seven died at Lexington ?
   Canst legibler write than Concord's large-stroked Act,
   Or when at Bunker Hill the clubbed guns cracked ?
   Hast ink more true than blood, or pen than fact ?
Nay, as the poet mad with heavenly fires
Flings men his song white-hot, then back retires,
Cools heart, broods o'er the song again, inquires,
   Why did I this, why that ? and slowly draws
   From Art's unconscious act Art's conscious laws ;
   So, Freedom, writ, declares her writing's cause.
All question vain, all chill foreboding vain.
Adams, ablaze with faith, is hot and fain ;
And he, straight-fibred Soul of mighty grain,
   Deep-rooted Washington, afire, serene—
   Tall Bush that burns, yet keeps its substance green—
   Sends daily word, of import calm yet keen,
Warm from the front of battle, till the fire
Wraps opposition in and flames yet higher,
And Doubt's thin tissues flash where Hope's aspire ;
   And, *Ay, declare,* and ever strenuous *Ay*
   Falls from the Twelve, and Time and Nature cry
   Consent with kindred burnings of July ;
And delegate Dead from each past age and race,
Viewless to man, in large procession pace
Downward athwart each set and steadfast face,
   Responding *Ay* in many tongues ; and lo !
   Manhood and Faith and Self and Love and Woe
   And Art and Brotherhood and Learning go
Rearward the files of dead, and softly say
Their saintly *Ay*, and softly pass away
By airy exits of that ample day.

Now fall the chill reactionary snows
Of man's defect, and every wind that blows
Keeps back the Spring of Freedom's perfect Rose.
Now naked feet with crimson fleck the ways,
And Heaven is stained with flags that mutinies raise,
And Arnold-spotted move the creeping days.
   Long do the eyes that look from Heaven see
   Time smoke, as in the spring the mulberry tree,
   With buds of battles opening fitfully,
Till Yorktown's winking vapors slowly fade,
And Time's full top casts down a pleasant shade
Where Freedom lies unarmed and unafraid.

———

Master, ever faster fly
Now the vivid seasons by ;
Now the glittering Western land
Twins the day-lit Eastern Strand ;
Now white Freedom's sea-bird wing
Roams the Sea of Everything ;
Now the freemen to and fro
Bind the tyrant sand and snow,
Snatching Death's hot bolt ere hurled,
Flash new Life about the world,
Sun the secrets of the hills,
Shame the gods' slow-grinding mills,
Prison Yesterday in Print,
Read To-morrow's weather-hint,
Haste before the halting Time,
Try new virtue and new crime,
Mould new faiths, devise new creeds,
Run each road that frontward leads,
Driven by an Onward-ache,
Scorning souls that circles make.

Now, O Sin! O Love's lost Shame!
Burns the land with redder flame :
North in line and South in line
Yell the charge and spring the mine.
Heartstrong South would have his way,
Headstrong North hath said him nay :
O strong Heart, strong Brain, beware!
Hear a Song from out the air :

I.

" Lists all white and blue in the skies;
    And the people hurried amain
  To the Tournament under the ladies' eyes
    Where jousted Heart and Brain.

II.

" *Blow, herald, blow !*   There entered Heart,
    A youth in crimson and gold.
  Blow, herald, blow !   Brain stood apart,
    Steel-armored, glittering, cold.

III.

" Heart's palfrey caracoled gayly round,
    Heart tra li-raed merrily ;
  But Brain sat still, with never a sound—
    Full cynical-calm was he.

IV.

" Heart's helmet-crest bore favors three
    From his lady's white hand caught ;
  Brain's casque was bare as Fact—not he
    Or favor gave or sought.

V.

" *Blow, herald, blow !* Heart shot a glance
   To catch his lady's eye ;
But Brain looked straight a-front, his lance
   To aim more faithfully.

VI.

" They charged, they struck ; both fell, both bled ;
   Brain rose again, ungloved ;
Heart fainting smiled, and softly said,
   My love to my Beloved."

   Heart and Brain ! no more be twain ;
   Throb and think, one flesh again !
   Lo ! they weep, they turn, they run ;
   Lo ! they kiss : Love, thou art one !

———

Now the Land, with drying tears,
Counts him up his flocks of years,
" See," he says, " my substance grows ;
Hundred-flocked my Herdsman goes,
Hundred-flocked my Herdsman stands
On the Past's broad meadow-lands,
Come from where ye mildly graze,
Black herds, white herds, nights and days.
Drive them homeward, Herdsman Time,
From the meadows of the Prime :
I will feast my house, and rest.
Neighbor East, come over West ;
Pledge me in good wine and words
While I count my hundred herds,

Sum the substance of my Past
From the first unto the last,
Chanting o'er the generous brim
Cloudy memories yet more dim,
Ghostly rhymes of Norsemen pale
Staring by old Björne's sail,
Strains more noble of that night
Worn Columbus saw his Light,
Psalms of still more heavenly tone,
How the Mayflower tossed alone,
Olden tale and later song
Of the Patriot's love and wrong,
Grandsire's ballad, nurse's hymn—
Chanting o'er the sparkling brim
Till I shall from first to last
Sum the substance of my Past."

———

Then called the Artist's God from in the sky :
" This Time shall show by dream and mystery
The heart of all his matter to thine eye.
Son, study stars by looking down in streams,
Interpret that which is by that which seems,
And tell thy dreams in words which are but dreams."

I.

The Master with His lucent hand
Pinched up the atom hills and plains
O'er all the moiety of land
The ocean-bounded West contains :
The dust lay dead upon the calm
And mighty middle of His palm.

II.

And lo! He wrought full tenderly,
And lo! He wrought with love and might,
    And lo! He wrought a thing to see
Was marvel in His people's sight:
    He wrought His image dead and small,
    A nothing fashioned like an All.

III.

    Then breathed He softly on the dead:
" Live Self!—thou part, yet none, of Me;
    Dust for humility," He said,
" And my warm breath for Charity.
    Behold my latest work, thou Earth!
    The Self of Man is taking birth."

IV.

    Then, Land, tall Adam of the West,
Thou stood'st upon the springy sod,
    Thy large eye ranging self-possest,
Thy limbs the limbs of God's young god,
    Thy Passion murmuring *I will*—
    Lord of the Lordship Good-and-Ill.

V.

    O manful arms, of supple size
To clasp a world or a waist as well!
    O manful eyes, to front the skies
Or look much pity down on hell!
    O manful tongue, to work and sing,
    And soothe a child and dare a king!

VI.

O wonder ! Now thou sleep'st in pain,
Like as some dream thy soul did grieve :
  God wounds thee, heals thee whole again,
And calls thee trembling to thine Eve.
  Wide-armed, thou dropp'st on knightly knee :
  Dear Love, Dear Freedom, go with me !

VII.

Then all the beasts before thee passed—
Beast War, Oppression, Murder, Lust,
  False Art, False Faith, slow skulking last—
And out of Time's thick-rising dust
  Thy Lord said, " Name them, tame them, Son ;
  Nor rest, nor rest, till thou hast done."

VIII.

Ah, name thou false, or tame thou wrong,
At heart let no man fear for thee :
  Thy Past sings ever Freedom's Song,
Thy Future's voice sounds wondrous free ;
  And Freedom is more large than Crime,
  And Error is more small than Time.

IX.

Come, thou whole Self of Latter Man !
Come o'er thy realm of Good-and-Ill,
  And do, thou Self that say'st *I can,*
And love, thou Self that say'st *I will ;*
  And prove and know Time's worst and best,
  Thou tall young Adam of the West !
BALTIMORE, 1876.

AT FIRST.

TO CHARLOTTE CUSHMAN.

MY crippled sense fares bow'd along
   His uncompanioned way,
And wronged by death pays life with wrong
And I wake by night and dream by day.

And the Morning seems but fatiguèd Night
   That hath wept his visage pale,
And the healthy mark 'twixt dark and light
In sickly sameness out doth fail.

And the woods stare strange, and the wind is dumb,
   —O Wind, pray talk again—
And the Hand of the Frost spreads stark and numb
As Death's on the deadened window-pane.

Still dumb, thou Wind, old voluble friend?
   And the middle of the day is cold,
And the heart of eve beats lax i' the end
As a legend's climax poorly told.

Oh vain the up straining of the hands
   In the chamber late at night,
Oh vain the complainings, the hot demands,
The prayers for a sound, the tears for a sight.

No word from over the starry line,
   No motion felt in the dark,
And never a day gives ever a sign
Or a dream sets seal with palpable mark.

And O my God, how slight it were,
   How nothing, thou All ! to thee,
That a kiss or a whisper might fall from her
Down by the way of Time to me :

Or some least grace of the body of love,
   —Mere wafture of floating-by,
Mere sense of unseen smiling above,
Mere hint sincere of a large blue eye,

Mere dim receipt of sad delight
   From Nearness warm in the air,
What time with the passing of the night
She also passed, somehow, somewhere.

BALTIMORE, 1876.

A BALLAD OF TREES AND THE MASTER.

INTO the woods my Master went,
Clean forspent, forspent.
Into the woods my Master came,
Forspent with love and shame.
But the olives they were not blind to Him,
The little gray leaves were kind to Him :
The thorn-tree had a mind to Him
When into the woods He came.

Out of the woods my Master went,
And He was well content.
Out of the woods my Master came,
Content with death and shame.
When Death and Shame would woo Him last,
From under the trees they drew Him last :
'Twas on a tree they slew Him—last
When out of the woods He came.

BALTIMORE, November, 1880.

A FLORIDA SUNDAY.

From cold Norse caves or buccaneer Southern seas
  Oft come repenting tempests here to die ;
Bewailing old-time wrecks and robberies,
  They shrive to priestly pines with many a sigh,
Breathe salutary balms through lank-lock'd hair
  Of sick men's heads, and soon—this world outworn—
Sink into saintly heavens of stirless air,
  Clean from confessional.   One died, this morn,
And willed the world to wise Queen Tranquil : she,
  Sweet sovereign Lady of all souls that bide
In contemplation, tames the too bright skies
  Like that faint agate film, far down descried.
Restraining suns in sudden thoughtful eyes
  Which flashed but now.   Blest distillation rare
Of o'er-rank brightness filtered waterwise
  Through all the earths in heaven—thou always fair,
Still virgin bride of e'er creating thought—
Dream-worker, in whose dream the Future's wrought—
Healer of hurts, free balm for bitter wrongs—
Most silent mother of all sounding songs—
Thou that dissolvest hells to make thy heaven—
Thou tempest's heir, that keep'st no tempest leaven—
But after winds' and thunders' wide mischance
Dost brood, and better thine inheritance—
Thou privacy of space, where each grave Star
As in his own still chamber sits afar

To meditate, yet, by thy walls unpent,
Shines to his fellows o'er the firmament—
Oh ! as thou liv'st in all this sky and sea
That likewise lovingly do live in thee,
So melt my soul in thee, and thine in me,
   Divine Tranquillity !

Gray Pelican, poised where yon broad shallows shine,
Know'st thou, that finny foison all is mine
In the bag below thy beak—yet thine, not less ?
For God, of His most gracious friendliness,
Hath wrought that every soul, this loving morn,
Into all things may be new-corporate born,
And each live whole in all : I sail with thee,
Thy Pelican's self is mine ; yea, silver Sea,
In this large moment all thy fishes, ripples, bights,
   Pale in-shore greens and distant blue delights,
   White visionary sails, long reaches fair
   By moon-horn'd strands that film the far-off air,
Bright sparkle-revelations, secret majesties,
   Shells, wrecks and wealths, are mine ; yea, Orange-trees,
   That lift your small world-systems in the light,
   Rich sets of round green heavens studded bright
   With globes of fruit that like still planets shine,
   Mine is your green-gold universe ; yea, mine,
   White slender Lighthouse fainting to the eye
   That wait'st on yon keen cape-point wistfully,
   Like to some maiden spirit pausing pale,
     New-wing'd, yet fain to sail
Above the serene Gulf to where a bridegroom soul
   Calls o'er the soft horizon—mine thy dole
   Of shut undaring wings and wan desire—
   Mine, too, thy later hope and heavenly fire
   Of kindling expectation ; yea, all sights,
     All sounds, that make this morn—quick flights

Of pea-green paroquets 'twixt neighbor trees,
Like missives and sweet morning inquiries
From green to green, in green—live oaks' round heads,
Busy with jays for thoughts—grays, whites and reds
Of pranked woodpeckers that ne'er gossip out,
But alway tap at doors and gad about—
Robins and mocking birds that all day long
Athwart straight sunshine weave cross-threads of song,
Shuttles of music—clouds of mosses gray
That rain me rains of pleasant thoughts alway
From a low sky of leaves—faint yearning psalms
Of endless metre breathing through the palms
That crowd and lean and gaze from off the shore
Ever for one that cometh nevermore—
Palmettos ranked, with childish spear-points set
Against no enemy—rich cones that fret
High roofs of temples shafted tall with pines—
Green, grateful mangroves where the sand-beach shines—
Long lissome coast that in and outward swerves,
The grace of God made manifest in curves—
All riches, goods and braveries never told
Of earth, sun, air and heaven—now I hold
Your being in my being ; I am ye,
 And ye myself ; yea, lastly, Thee,
God, whom my roads all reach, howe'er they run,
My Father, Friend, Belovèd, dear All-One,
Thee in my soul, my soul in Thee, I feel,
Self of my self. Lo, through my sense doth steal
Clear cognizance of all selves and qualities,
Of all existence that hath been or is,
Of all strange haps that men miscall of chance,
And all the works of tireless circumstance :
Each borders each, like mutual sea and shore,
Nor aught misfits his neighbor that 's before,

Nor him that 's after—nay, through this still air,
Out of the North come quarrels, and keen blare
Of challenge by the hot-breath'd parties blown ;
Yet break they not this peace with alien tone,
Fray not my heart, nor fright me for my land,
—I hear from all-wards, allwise understand,
The great bird Purpose bears me twixt her wings,
And I am one with all the kinsmen things
That e'er my Father fathered.   Oh, to me
All questions solve in this tranquillity :
E'en this dark matter, once so dim, so drear,
Now shines upon my spirit heavenly-clear:
Thou, Father, without logic, tellest me ·
How this divine denial true may be,
—How *All 's in each, yet every one of all*
Maintains his Self complete and several.

TAMPA, FLORIDA, 1877.

7

TO MY CLASS:

ON CERTAIN FRUITS AND FLOWERS SENT ME IN SICKNESS.

IF spicy-fringéd pinks that blush and pale
  With passions of perfume,—if violets blue
  That hint of heaven with odor more than hue,—
If perfect roses, each a holy Grail
Wherefrom the blood of beauty doth exhale
  Grave raptures round,—if leaves of green as new
  As those fresh chaplets wove in dawn and dew
By Emily when down the Athenian vale
She paced, to do observance to the May,
  Nor dreamed of Arcite nor of Palamon,—
If fruits that riped in some more riotous play
  Of wind and beam than stirs our temperate sun,—
    If these the products be of love and pain,
    Oft may I suffer, and you love, again.

BALTIMORE, Christmas, 1880.

ON VIOLET'S WAFERS,

SENT ME WHEN I WAS ILL.

FINE-TISSUED as her finger-tips, and white
   As all her thoughts; in shape like shields of prize,
   As if before young Violet's dreaming eyes
Still blazed the two great Theban bucklers bright
That swayed the random of that furious fight
   Where Palamon and Arcite made assize
   For Emily; fresh, crisp as her replies,
That, not with sting, but pith, do oft invite
   More trial of the tongue; simple, like her,
Well fitting lowlihood, yet fine as well,
   —The queen's no finer; rich (though gossamer)
In help to him they came to, which may tell
     How rich that him *she'll* come to; thus men see,
     Like Violet's self e'en Violet's wafers be.

BALTIMORE, 1881.

IRELAND.

WRITTEN FOR THE ART AUTOGRAPH DURING THE IRISH
FAMINE, 1880.

HEARTSOME Ireland, winsome Ireland,
  Charmer of the sun and sea,
Bright beguiler of old anguish,
  How could Famine frown on thee ?

As our Gulf-Stream, drawn to thee-ward,
  Turns him from his northward flow,
And our wintry western headlands
  Send thee summer from their snow,

Thus the main and cordial current
  Of our love sets over sea,—
Tender, comely, valiant Ireland,
Songful, soulful, sorrowful Ireland,—
  Streaming warm to comfort thee.

BALTIMORE, 1880.

UNDER THE CEDARCROFT CHESTNUT.

TRIM set in ancient sward, his manful bole
　　Upbore his frontage largely toward the sky.
We could not dream but that he had a soul :
　　What virtue breathed from out his bravery !

We gazed o'erhead : far down our deepening eyes
　　Rained glamours from his green midsummer mass.
The worth and sum of all his centuries
　　Suffused his mighty shadow on the grass.

A Presence large, a grave and steadfast Form
　　Amid the leaves' light play and fantasy,
A calmness conquered out of many a storm,
　　A Manhood mastered by a chestnut-tree !

Then, while his monarch fingers downward held
　　The rugged burrs wherewith his state was rife,
A voice of large authoritative Eld
　　Seemed uttering quickly parables of life :

How Life in truth was sharply set with ills ;
　　A kernel cased in quarrels ; yea, a sphere
Of stings, and hedge-hog-round of mortal quills :
　　How most men itched to eat too soon i' the year,

And took but wounds and worries for their pains,
　　Whereas the wise withheld their patient hands,
Nor plucked green pleasures till the sun and rains
　　And seasonable ripenings burst all bands

And opened wide the liberal burrs of life.
   There, O my Friend, beneath the chestnut bough,
Gazing on thee immerged in modern strife,
   I framed a prayer of fervency—that thou,

In soul and stature larger than thy kind,
   Still more to this strong Form might'st liken thee,
Till thy whole Self in every fibre find
   The tranquil lordship of thy chestnut tree.

TAMPA, FLORIDA, February, 1877.

EVENING SONG.

Look off, dear Love, across the sallow sands,
  And mark yon meeting of the sun and sea,
How long they kiss in sight of all the lands.
      Ah ! longer, longer, we.

Now in the sea's red vintage melts the sun,
  As Egypt's pearl dissolved in rosy wine,
And Cleopatra night drinks all. 'Tis done,
      Love, lay thine hand in mine.

Come forth, sweet stars, and comfort heaven's heart ;
  Glimmer, ye waves, round else unlighted sands.
O night ! divorce our sun and sky apart
      Never our lips, our hands.

1876.

A SUNRISE SONG.

Young palmer sun, that to these shining sands
   Pourest thy pilgrim's tale, discoursing still
Thy silver passages of sacred lands,
   With news of Sepulchre and Dolorous Hill,

Canst thou be he that, yester-sunset warm,
   Purple with Paynim rage and wrack desire,
Dashed ravening out of a dusty lair of Storm,
   Harried the west, and set the world on fire?

Hast thou perchance repented, Saracen Sun?
   Wilt warm the world with peace and dove-desire?
Or wilt thou, ere this very day be done,
   Blaze Saladin still, with unforgiving fire?

Baltimore 1881.

---

[1] "A Sunrise Song" leads a group of seven short poems over-looked in earlier editions. Six of these, beginning with "On A Palmetto," were unrevised pencillings of late date, excepting the lines of 1866 to J. D. H.

ON A PALMETTO.

THROUGH all that year-scarred agony of height,
Unblest of bough or bloom, to where expands
His wandy circlet with his bladed bands
Dividing every wind, or loud or light,
To termless hymns of love and old despite,
Yon tall palmetto in the twilight stands,
Bare Dante of these purgatorial sands
That glimmer marginal to the monstrous night.
Comes him a Southwind from the scented vine,
It breathes of Beatrice through all his blades,
North, East or West, Guelph-wind or Ghibelline
'Tis shredded into music down the shades ;
All sea-breaths, land-breaths, systol, diastol,
Sway, minstrels of that grief-melodious Soul.

1880.

STRUGGLE.

My soul is like the oar that momently
   Dies in a desperate stress beneath the wave,
Then glitters out again and sweeps the sea :
   Each second I'm new-born from some new grave.

CONTROL.

O HUNGER, Hunger, I will harness thee
And make thee harrow all my spirit's glebe.
Of old the blind bard Hervé sang so sweet
He made a wolf to plow his land.

TO J. D. H.

(KILLED AT SURREY C. H., OCTOBER, 1866.)

.　　.　　.　　.　　.　　.

DEAR friend, forgive a wild lament
　　Insanely following thy flight.
I would not cumber thine ascent
　　Nor drag thee back into the night;

But the great sea-winds sigh with me,
　　The fair-faced stars seem wrinkled, old,
And l would that I might lie with thee
　　There in the grave so cold, so cold !

Grave walls are thick, I cannot see thee,
　　And the round skies are far and steep;
A-wild to quaff some cup of Lethe,
　　Pain is proud and scorns to weep.

My heart breaks if it cling about thee,
　　And still breaks, if far from thine.
O drear, drear death, to live without thee,
　　O sad life—to keep thee mine.

.　　.　　.　　.　　.　　.

MARSH HYMNS.

BETWEEN DAWN AND SUNRISE.

WERE silver pink, and had a soul,
   Which soul were shy, which shyness might
A visible influence be, and roll
   Through heaven and earth—'twere thou, O light!

O rhapsody of the wraith of red,
   O blush but yet in prophecy,
O sun-hint that hath overspread
   Sky, marsh, my soul, and yonder sail.

THOU AND I.

So one in heart and thought, I trow,
That thou might'st press the strings and I might draw the
    bow
And both would meet in music sweet,
Thou and I, I trow.

  1881.

THE HARD TIMES IN ELFLAND.

A STORY OF CHRISTMAS EVE.

STRANGE that the termagant winds should scold
    The Christmas Eve so bitterly!
But Wife, and Harry the four-year-old,
    Big Charley, Nimblewits, and I,

Blithe as the wind was bitter, drew
    More frontward of the mighty fire,
Where wise Newfoundland Fan foreknew
    The heaven that Christian dogs desire—

Stretched o'er the rug, serene and grave,
    Huge nose on heavy paws reclined,
With never a drowning boy to save,
    And warmth of body and peace of mind.

And, as our happy circle sat,
    The fire well capp'd the company:
In grave debate or careless chat,
    A right good fellow, mingled he:

He seemed as one of us to sit,
    And talked of things above, below,
With flames more winsome than our wit,
    And coals that burned like love aglow.

While thus our rippling discourse rolled
  Smooth down the channel of the night,
We spoke of Time : thereat, one told
  A parable of the Seasons' flight.

" Time was a Shepherd with four sheep.
  In a certain Field he long abode.
He stood by the bars, and his flock bade leap
  One at a time to the Common Road.

" And first there leapt, like bird on wing,
  A lissome Lamb that played in the air.
I heard the Shepherd call him *Spring :*
  Oh, large-eyed, fresh and snowy fair

" He skipped the flowering Highway fast,
  Hurried tne hedgerows green and white,
Set maids and men a-yearning, passed
  The Bend, and gamboll'd out of sight.

" And next marched forth a matron Ewe
  (While Time took down a bar for her),
Udder'd so large 'twas much ado
  E'en then to clear the barrier.

" Full softly shone her silken fleece
  What stately time she paced along :
Each heartsome hoof-stroke wrought increase
  Of sunlight, substance, seedling, song,

" In flower, in fruit, in field, in bird,
  Till the great globe, rich fleck'd and pied,
Like some large peach half pinkly furred,
  Turned to the sun a glowing side
  7*

" And hung in the heavenly orchard, bright,
    None-such, complete.
                        Then, while the Ewe
  Slow passed the Bend, a blur of light,
    The Shepherd's face in sadness grew :

" ' Summer ! ' he said, as one would say
    A sigh in syllables. So, in haste
(For shame of Summer's long delay,
    Yet gazing still what way she paced),

" He summoned Autumn, slanting down
    The second bar. Thereover strode
A Wether, fleeced in burning brown,
    And largely loitered down the Road.

" Far as the farmers sight his shape
    Majestic moving o'er the way,
All cry *To harvest*, crush the grape,
    And haul the corn and house the hay,

" Till presently, no man can say,
    (So brown the woods that line that end)
If yet the brown-fleeced Wether may,
    Or not, have passed beyond the Bend.

" Now turn I towards the Shepherd : lo,
    An aged Ram, flapp'd, gnarly-horn'd,
With bones that crackle o'er the snow,
    Rheum'd, wind-gall'd, rag-fleec'd, burr'd and thorn'd !

" Time takes the third bar off for him,
    He totters down the windy lane.
'Tis Winter, still : the Bend lies dim.
    O Lamb, would thou wouldst leap **again** !"

Those seasons out, we talked of these :
    And I (with inward purpose sly
To shield my purse from Christmas trees
    And stockings and wild robbery

When Hal and Nimblewits invade
    My cash in Santa Claus's name)
In full the hard, hard times surveyed ;
    Denounced all waste as crime and shame ;

Hinted that " waste " might be a term
    Including skates, velocipedes,
Kites, marbles, soldiers, towers infirm,
    Bows, arrows, cannon, Indian reeds,

Cap-pistols, drums, mechanic toys,
    And all th' infernal host of horns
Whereby to strenuous hells of noise
    Are turned the blessed Christmas morns ;

Thus, roused—those horns !—to sacred rage,
    I rose, forefinger high in air,
When Harry cried (*some* war to wage),
    " Papa, is hard times ev'ywhere ?

" Maybe in Santa Claus's land
    It isn't hard times none at all ! "
Now, blessed Vision ! to my hand
    Most pat, a marvel strange did fall.

Scarce had my Harry ceased, when " Look ! "
    He cried, leapt up in wild alarm,
Ran to my Comrade, shelter took
    Beneath the startled mother's arm.

And so was still : what time we saw
   A foot hang down the fireplace ! Then,
With painful sciambling scratched and raw,
   Two hands that seemed like hands of men

Eased down two legs and a body through
   The blazing fire, and forth there came
Before our wide and wondering view
   A figure shrinking half with shame,

And half with weakness.   " Sir," I said,
   —But with a mien of dignity
The seedy stranger raised his head :
   " My friends, I 'm Santa Claus," said he.

But oh, how changed !   That rotund face
   The new moon rivall'd, pale and thin ;
Where once was cheek, now empty space ;
   Whate'er stood out, did now stand in.

His piteous legs scarce propped him up :
   His arms mere sickles seemed to be :
But most o'erflowed our sorrow's cup
   When that we saw—or did not see—

His belly : we remembered how
   It shook like a bowl of jelly fine :
An earthquake could not shake it now ;
   He *had* no belly—not a sign.

" Yes, yes, old friends, you well may stare :
   I *have* seen better days," he said :
" But now, with shrinkage, loss and care,
   Your Santa Claus scarce owns his head.

" We've had such hard, hard times this year
    For goblins ! Never knew the like.
All Elfland's mortgaged ! And we fear
    The gnomes are just about to strike.

" I once was rich, and round, and hale.
    The whole world called me jolly brick ;
But listen to a piteous tale.
    Young Harry,—Santa Claus is sick !

" 'Twas thus : a smooth-tongued railroad man
    Comes to my house and talks to me :
' *I 've got,*' says he, ' *a little plan*
    That suits this nineteenth century.

" ' *Instead of driving, as you do,*
    Six reindeer slow from house to house,
Let 's build a Grand Trunk Railway through
    From here to earth's last terminus.

" ' *We 'll touch at every chimney-top*
    (An Elevated Track, of course),
Then, as we whisk you by, you'll drop
    Each package down : just think, the force

" ' *You 'll save, the time !—Besides, we 'll make*
    Our millions : look you, soon we will
Compete for freights—and then we 'll take
    Dame Fortune's bales of good and ill

" ' *(Why, she 's the biggest shipper, sir,*
    That e'er did business in this world !) :
Then Death, that ceaseless Traveller,
    Shall on his rounds by us be whirled.

" ' *When ghosts return to walk with men,*
        We'll bring 'em cheap by steam, and fast:
    We'll run a Branch to heaven! and then
        We'll riot, man; for then, at last

" ' *We'll make with heaven a contract fair*
        To call, each hour, from town to town,
    And carry the dead folks' souls up there,
        And bring the unborn babies down! '

" The plan seemed fair: I gave him cash,
        Nay, every penny I could raise.
    My wife e'er cried, ' *'Tis rash, 'tis rash:* '
        How could I know the stock-thief's ways?

" But soon I learned full well, poor fool!
        My woes began, that wretched day.
    The President plied me like a tool.
        In lawyer's fees, and rights of way,

" Injunctions, leases, charters, I
        Was meshed as in a mighty maze.
    The stock ran low, the talk ran high:
        Then quickly flamed the final blaze.

" With never an inch of track—'tis true!
        The debts were large . . . the oft-told tale.
    The President rolled in splendor new
        —He bought my silver at the sale.

" Yes, sold me out: we've moved away.
        I've had to give up everything.
    My reindeer, even, whom I . . . pray,
        Excuse me " . . . here, o'er-sorrowing,

Poor Santa Claus burst into tears,
    Then calmed again : " my reindeer fleet,
I gave them up : on foot, my dears,
    I now must plod through snow and sleet.

" Retrenchment rules in Elfland, now ;
    Yes, every luxury is cut off.
   —Which, by the way, reminds me how
    I caught this dreadful hacking cough :

" I cut off the tail of my Ulster furred
    To make young Kris a coat of state.
That very night the storm occurred !
    Thus we become the sport of Fate.

" For I was out till after one,
    Surveying chimney-tops and roofs,
And planning how it could be done
    Without my reindeers' bouncing hoofs.

" ' *My dear*,' says Mrs. Claus, that night
    (A most superior woman she !)
 ' *It never, never can be right*
    That you, deep-sunk in poverty,

" ' *This year should leave your poor old bed,*
    And trot about, bent down with toys,
(There's Kris a-crying now for bread !)
    To give to other people's boys.

" ' *Since you've been out, the news arrives*
    The Elfs' Insurance Company's gone.
Ah, Claus, those premiums !   Now, our lives
    Depend on yours : thus griefs go on.

" ' *And even while you're thus harassed,*
   I do believe, if out you went,
   You'd go, in spite of all that's passed,
   To the children of that President ! '

" Oh, Charley, Harry, Nimblewits,
   These eyes, that night, ne'er slept a wink.
My path seemed honeycombed with pits.
   Naught could I do but think and think.

" But, with the day, my courage rose.
   Ne'er shall my boys, *my* boys (I cried),
When Christmas morns their eyes unclose,
   Find empty stockings gaping wide !

" Then hewed and whacked and whittled I ;
   The wife, the girls and Kris took fire ;
They spun, sewed, cut,—till by and by
   We made, at home, my pack entire ! "

(He handed me a bundle, here.)
   " Now, hoist me up : there, gently : quick !
Dear boys, *don't* look for much this year :
   Remember, Santa Claus is sick ! "

BALTIMORE, December, 1877.

DIALECT POEMS.

A FLORIDA GHOST.

Down mildest shores of milk-white sand,
  By cape and fair Floridian bay,
Twixt billowy pines—a surf asleep on land—
  And the great Gulf at play,

Past far-off palms that filmed to nought,
  Or in and out the cunning keys
That laced the land like fragile patterns wrought
  To edge old broideries,

The sail sighed on all day for joy,
  The prow each pouting wave did leave
All smile and song, with sheen and ripple coy,
  Till the dusk diver Eve

Brought up from out the brimming East
  The oval moon, a perfect pearl.
In that large lustre all our haste surceased,
  The sail seemed fain to furl,

The silent steersman landward turned,
  And ship and shore set breast to breast.
Under a palm wherethrough a planet burned
  We ate, and sank to rest.

But soon from sleep's dear death (it seemed)
  I rose and strolled along the sea
Down silver distances that faintly gleamed
  On to infinity.

Till suddenly I paused, for lo !
    A shape (from whence I ne'er divined)
Appeared before me, pacing to and fro,
    With head far down inclined.

A wraith (I thought) *that walks the shore*
    To solve some old perplexity.
Full heavy hung the draggled gown he wore ;
    His hair flew all awry.

He waited·not (as ghosts oft use)
    To be *dearheaven'd !* and *oh'd !*
But briskly said : " Good-evenin' ; what 's the news ?
    Consumption ?   After boa'd ?

" Or mebbe you 're intendin' of
    Investments ?   Orange-plantin' ?   Pine ?
Hotel ? or Sanitarium ?   What above
    This yea'th *can* be your line ?

" Speakin' of sanitariums, now,
    Jest look 'ee here, my friend :
I know a little story,—well, I swow,
    Wait till you hear the end !

" Some year or more ago, I s'pose,
    I roamed from Maine to Floridy,
And,—see where them Palmettos grows ?
    I bought that little key,

" Cal'latin' for to build right off
    A c'lossal sanitarium :
Big surf !   Gulf breeze !   Jest death upon a cough !
    —I run it high, to hum !

" Well, sir, I went to work in style:
    Bought me a steamboat, loaded it
With my hotel (pyazers more 'n a mile !)
    Already framed and fit,

" Insured 'em, fetched 'em safe around,
    Put up my buildin', moored my boat,
Com-plete ! then went to bed and slept as sound
    As if I 'd paid a note.

" Now on that very night a squall,
    Cum up from some'eres—some bad place !
An' blowed an' tore an' reared an' pitched an' all,
    —I had to run a race

" Right out o' bed from that hotel
    An' git to yonder risin' ground,
For, 'twixt the sea that riz and rain that fell,
    I pooty nigh was drowned !

" An' thar I stood till mornin' cum,
    Right on yon little knoll of sand,
Fre*quent*ly wishin' I had stayed to hum
    Fur from this tarnal land.

" When mornin' cum, I took a good
    Long look, and—well, sir, sure 's I 'm *me*—
That boat laid right whar that hotel had stood,
    And *hit* sailed out to sea!

" No : I'll not keep you : good-bye, friend.
    Don't think about it much,—preehaps
Your brain might git see-sawin', end for end,
    Like them asylum chaps,

" For here *I* walk, forevermore,
    A-tryin' to make it gee,
How one same wind could blow my ship to shore
    And mv hotel to sea ! "

CHADD'S FORD, PENNSYLVANIA, 1877.

UNCLE JIM'S BAPTIST REVIVAL HYMN.

BY SIDNEY AND CLIFFORD LANIER.

[Not long ago a certain Georgia cotton-planter, driven to despera-
tion by awaking each morning to find that the grass had quite out-
grown the cotton overnight, and was likely to choke it, in defiance of
his lazy freedmen's hoes and ploughs, set the whole State in a laugh by
exclaiming to a group of fellow-sufferers : " It's all stuff about Cincin-
natus leaving the plough to go into politics *for patriotism ;* he was just
a-runnin' from grass ! "
This state of things—when the delicate young rootlets of the cotton
are struggling against the hardier multitudes of the grass-suckers—is
universally described in plantation parlance by the phrase " in the
grass ; " and Uncle Jim appears to have found in it so much similarity
to the condition of his own (" Baptis' ") church, overrun, as it was, by
the cares of this world, that he has embodied it in the refrain of a re-
vival hymn such as the colored improvisator of the South not infre-
quently constructs from his daily surroundings.   He has drawn all the
ideas of his stanzas from the early morning phenomena of those critical
weeks when the loud plantation-horn is blown before daylight, in order
to rouse all hands for a long day's fight against the common enemy of
cotton-planting mankind.
In addition to these exegetical commentaries, the Northern reader
probably needs to be informed that the phrase " peerten up " means
substantially *to spur up,* and is an active form of the adjective " peert "
(probably a corruption of *pert*), which is so common in the South, and
which has much the signification of " smart " in New England, as *e.g.*,
a " peert " horse, in antithesis to a " sorry "—*i.e.*, poor, mean, lazy one.]

Solo.—Sin's rooster 's crowed, Ole Mahster 's riz,
　　　De sleepin'-time is pas' ;
　　Wake up dem lazy Baptissis,
Chorus.—*Dey 's mightily in de grass, grass,*
　　　Dey 's mightily in de grass.

　　Ole Mahster 's blowed de mornin' horn,
　　　He 's blowed a powerful blas' :
　　O Baptis' come, come hoe de corn,
　　　You 's mightily in de grass, grass,
　　　You 's mightily in de grass.

De Meth'dis team's done hitched ; O fool,
  De day's a-breakin' fas' ;
Gear up dat lean ole Baptis' mule,
    Dey's mightily in de grass, grass,
    Dey's mightily in de grass.

De workmen's few an' mons'rous slow,
  De cotton's sheddin' fas' ;
Whoop, look, jes' look at de Baptis' row,
    Hit's mightily in de grass, grass,
    Hit's mightily in de grass.

De jay-bird squeal to de mockin'-bird : "Stop !
  Don' gimme none o' yo' sass ;
Better sing one song for de Baptis' crop,
    Dey's mightily in de grass, grass,
    Dey's mightily in de grass."

And de ole crow croak : "Doh' work, no, no ; "
  But de fiel'-lark say, " Yaas, yaas,
An' I spec' you mighty glad,   u debblish crow,
    Dat de Baptissis's in de grass, grass,
    Dat de Baptissis's in de grass ! "

Lord, thunder us up to de plowin'-match,
  Lord, peerten de hoein' fas',
Yea, Lord, hab mussy en de Baptis' patch,
    Dey's mightily in de grass, grass,
    Dey's mightily in de grass.

1876.

NINE FROM EIGHT.

I WAS drivin' my two-mule waggin,
With a lot o' truck for sale,
Towards Macon, to git some baggin'
(Which my cotton was ready to bale),
And I come to a place on the side o' the pike
Whar a peert little winter branch jest had throw'd
The sand in a kind of a sand-bar like,
And I seed, a leetle ways up the road,
A man squattin' down, like a big bull-toad,
On the ground, a-figgerin' thar in the sand
With his finger, and motionin' with his hand,
    And he looked like Ellick Garry.
And as I driv up, I heerd him bleat
To hisself, like a lamb : " Hauh ? nine from eight
    Leaves nuthin'—and none to carry ? "

And Ellick's bull-cart was standin'
A cross-wise of the way,
And the little bull was a-expandin',
Hisself on a wisp of hay.
But Ellick he sat with his head bent down,
A-studyin' and musin' powerfully,
And his forrud was creased with a turrible frown,
And he was a-wurken' appearently
A 'rethmetic sum that wouldn't gee,
  8

Fur he kep' on figgerin' away in the sand
With his finger, and motionin' with his hand,
        And I seed it *was* Ellick Garry.
And agin I heard him softly bleat
To hisself, like a lamb : " Hauh ? nine from eight
        Leaves nuthin'—and none to carry ! "

I woa'd my mules mighty easy
(Ellick's back was towards the road
And the wind hit was sorter breezy)
And I got down off'n my load,
And I crep' up close to Ellick's back,
And I heerd him a-talkin' softly, thus :
" Them figgers is got me under the hack.
I caint see how to git out'n the muss,
Except to jest nat'ally fail and bus' !
My crap-leen calls for nine hundred and more.
My counts o' sales is eight hundred and four,
        Of cotton for Ellick Garry.
Thar's eight, ought, four, jest like on a slate :
Here's nine and two oughts—Hauh ? nine from eight
        Leaves nuthin'—and none to carry.

" Them crap-leens, oh, them crap-leens !
I giv one to Pardman and Sharks.
Hit gobbled me up like snap-beans
In a patch full o' old fiel'-larks.
But I thought I could fool the crap-leen nice,
And I hauled my cotton to Jammel and Cones.
But shuh ! 'fore I even had settled my price
They tuck affidavy without no bones
And levelled upon me fur all ther loans
To the 'mount of sum nine hundred dollars or more,
And sold me out clean for eight hundred and four,

As sure as I'm Ellick Garry !
And thar it is down all squar and straight,
But I can't make it gee, fur nine from eight
 Leaves nuthin'—and none to carry."

Then I says " Hello, here, Garry !
However you star' and frown
Thare 's somethin' fur *you* to carry,
Fur you 've worked it upside down ! "
Then he riz and walked to his little bull-cart,
And made like he neither had seen nor heerd
Nor knowed that I knowed of his raskilly part,
And he tried to look as if *he* wa'nt feared,
And gathered his lines like he never keered,
And he driv down the road 'bout a quarter or so,
And then looked around, and I hollered " Hello,
 Look here, Mister Ellick Garry !
You may git up soon and lie down late,
But you'll always find that nine from eight
 Leaves nuthin'—and none to carry."

Macon, Georgia, 1870.

THAR 'S MORE IN THE MAN THAN THAR IS IN THE LAND.

I KNOWED a man, which he lived in Jones,
Which Jones is a county of red hills and stones,
And he lived pretty much by gittin' of loans,
And his mules was nuthin' but skin and bones,
And his hogs was flat as his corn-bread pones,
And he had 'bout a thousand acres o' land.

This man—which his name it was also Jones—
He swore that he 'd leave them old red hills and stones,
Fur he couldn't make nuthin' but yallerish cotton,
And little o' *that*, and his fences was rotten,
And what little corn he had, *hit* was boughten
And dinged ef a livin' was in the land.

And the longer he swore the madder he got,
And he riz and he walked to the stable lot,
And he hollered to Tom to come thar and hitch
Fur to emigrate somewhar whar land was rich,
And to quit raisin' cock-burrs, thistles and sich,
And a wastin' ther time on the cussed land.

So him and Tom they hitched up the mules,
Pertestin' that folks was mighty big fools
That 'ud stay in Georgy ther lifetime out,
Jest scratchin' a livin' when all of 'em mought
Git places in Texas whar cotton would sprout
By the time you could plant it in the land.

And he driv by a house whar a man named Brown
Was a livin', not fur from the edge o' town,
And he bantered Brown fur to buy his place,
And said that bein' as money was skace,
And bein' as sheriffs was hard to face,
Two dollars an acre would git the land.

They closed at a dollar and fifty cents,
And Jones he bought him a waggin and tents,
And loaded his corn, and his wimmin, and truck,
And moved to Texas, which it tuck
His entire pile, with the best of luck,
To git thar and git him a little land.

But Brown moved out on the old Jones' farm,
And he rolled up his breeches and bared his arm,
And he picked all the rocks from off'n the groun',
And he rooted it up and he plowed it down,
Then he sowed his corn and his wheat in the land.

Five years glid by, and Brown, one day
(Which he 'd got so fat that he wouldn't weigh),
Was a settin' down, sorter lazily,
To the bulliest dinner you ever see,
When one o' the children jumped on his knee
And says, " Yan 's Jones, which you bought his land."

And thar was Jones, standin' out at the fence,
And he hadn't no waggin, nor mules, nor tents,
Fur he had left Texas afoot and cum
To Georgy to see if he couldn't git sum
Employment, and he was a lookin' as hum-
Ble as ef he had never owned any land.

But Brown he axed him in, and he sot
Him down to his vittles smokin' hot,
And when he had filled hisself and the floor
Brown looked at him sharp and riz and swore
That, "whether men's land was rich or poor
Thar was more in the *man* than thar was in the *land*."

MACON, GEORGIA, 1869.

JONES'S PRIVATE ARGYMENT.

THAT air same Jones, which lived in Jones,
    He had this pint about him :
He'd swear with a hundred sighs and groans,
That farmers *must* stop gittin' loans,
    And git along without 'em :

That bankers, warehousemen, and sich
    Was fatt'nin' on the planter,
And Tennessy was rotten-rich
A-raisin' meat and corn, all which
    Draw'd money to Atlanta :

And the only thing (says Jones) to do
    Is, eat no meat that 's boughten :
But tear up every I, O, U,
And plant all corn and swear for true
    To quit a-raisin' cotton !

Thus spouted Jones (whar folks could hear,
    —At Court and other gatherin's),
And thus kep' spoutin' many a year,
Proclaimin' loudly far and near
    Sich fiddlesticks and blatherin's.

But, one all-fired sweatin' day,
    It happened I was hoein'
My lower corn-field, which it lay
'Longside the road that runs my way
    Whar I can see what's goin'.

And a'ter twelve o'clock had come
    I felt a kinder faggin',
And laid myself un'neath a plum
To let my dinner settle sum,
    When 'long come Jones's waggin,

And Jones was settin' in it, *so :*
    A-readin' of a paper.
His mules was goin' powerful slow,
Fur he had tied the lines onto
    The staple of the scraper.

The mules they stopped about a rod
    From me, and went to feedin'
'Longside the road, upon the sod,
But Jones (which he had tuck a tod)
    Not knowin', kept a-readin'.

And presently says he : " Hit's true ;
    That Clisby's head is level.
Thar's one thing farmers all must do,
To keep themselves from goin' tew
    Bankruptcy and the devil !

" More corn ! more corn ! *must* plant less ground,
    And *mustn't* eat what's boughten !
Next year they'll do it : reasonin's sound :
(And, cotton will fetch 'bout a dollar a pound),
    Tharfore, I'll plant *all* cotton ! "

MACON, GEORGIA, 1870.

THE POWER OF PRAYER; OR, THE FIRST STEAMBOAT UP THE ALABAMA.

BY SIDNEY AND CLIFFORD LANIER.

You, Dinah! Come and set me whar de ribber-roads does
    meet.
De Lord, *He* made dese black-jack roots to twis' into a seat.
Umph, dar! De Lord have mussy on dis blin' ole nigger's
    feet.

It 'pear to me dis mornin' I kin smell de fust o' June.
I 'clar', I b'lieve dat mockin'-bird could play de fiddle soon !
Dem yonder town-bells sounds like dey was ringin' in de
    moon.

Well, ef dis nigger *is* been blind for fo'ty year or mo',
Dese ears, *dey* sees the world, like, th'u' de cracks dat's in
    de do'.
For de Lord has built dis body wid de windows 'hind and 'fo'.

I know my front ones *is* stopped up, and things is sort o'
    dim,
But den, th'u' *dem*, temptation's rain won't leak in on ole
    Jim !
De back ones show me earth enough, aldo' dey 's mons'ous
    slim.

And as for Hebben,—bless de Lord, and praise His holy
    name—
Dat shines in all de co'ners of dis cabin jes' de same
As ef dat cabin hadn't nar' a plank upon de frame !
    8*

Who *call* me ?   Listen down de ribber, Dinah !   Don't you
    hyar
Somebody holl'in' " *Hoo, Jim, hoo?* "   My Sarah died las'
    y'ar ;
Is dat black angel done come back to call ole Jim f om hyar ?

My stars, dat cain't be Sarah, shuh !   Jes' listen, Dinah, *now!*
What *kin* be comin' up dat bend, a-makin' sich a row ?
Fus' bellerin' like a pawin' bull, den squealin' like a sow ?

De Lord 'a' mussy sakes alive, jes' hear,—ker-woof, ker-
    woof—
De Debble 's comin' round dat bend, he 's comin' shuh enuff,
A-splashin' up de water wid his tail and wid his hoof !

I'se pow'ful skeered ; but neversomeless I ain't gwine run
    away :
I 'm gwine to stand stiff-legged for de Lord dis blessèd day.
You screech, and swish de water, Satan !   I 'se a gwine to
    pray.

O hebbenly Marster, what thou willest, dat mus' be jes' so,
And ef Thou hast bespoke de word, some nigger 's bound to
    go.
Den, Lord, please take ole Jim, and lef young Dinah hyar
    below !

'Scuse Dinah, 'scuse her, Marster ; for she 's sich a little chile,
She hardly jes' begin to scramble up de homeyard stile,
But dis ole traveller's feet been tired dis many a many a mile.

I'se wufless as de rotten pole of las' year's fodder-stack.
De rheumatiz done bit my bones ; you hear 'em crack and
    crack ?
I cain'st sit down 'dout gruntin' like 'twas breakin' o' my
    back.

What use de wheel, when hub and spokes is warped and
    split, and rotten ?
What use dis dried-up cotton-stalk, when Life done picked
    my cotton ?
I'se like a word dat somebody said, and den done been for-
    gotten.

But, Dinah !   Shuh dat gal jes' like dıs little hick'ry tree,
De sap 's jes' risin in her ; she do grow owdaciouslee—
Lord, ef you 's clarin' de underbrush, don't cut her down, cut
    me !

I would not proud persume—but I'll boldly make reques' ;
Sence Jacob had dat wrastlin'-match, I, too, gwine do my
    bes' ;
When Jacob got all underholt, de Lord he answered Yes !

And what for waste de vittles, now, and th'ow away de
    bread,
Jes' for to strength dese idle hands to scratch dis ole bald
    head ?
T'ink of de 'conomy, Marster, ef dis ole Jim was dead !

Stop ;—ef I don't believe de Debble 's gone on up de stream !
Jes' now he squealed down dar ;—hush ; dat's a mighty
    weakly scream !
Yas, sir, he 's gone, he 's gone ;—he snort way off, like in a
    dream !

O glory hallelujah to de Lord dat reigns on high !
De Debble 's fai'ly skeered to def, he done gone flyin' by ;
I know'd he couldn' stand dat pra'r, I felt my Marster
    nigh !

You, Dinah ; ain't you 'shamed, now, dat you didn' trust to
    grace ?
I heerd you thrashin' th'u' de bushes when he showed his
    face !
You fool, you think de Debble couldn't beat *you* in a race?

I tell you, Dinah, jes' as shuh as you is standin' dar,
When folks starts prayin', answer-angels drops down th'u'
    de a'r.
Yas, Dinah, whar'ould you be now, jes' 'ceptin' fur dat pra'r ?

BALTIMORE, 1875.

UNREVISED EARLY POEMS.

These unrevised poems are not necessarily exponents of Mr. Lanier's later teaching, but are offered as examples of his youthful spirit, his earlier methods and his instructive growth. To many friends they present in addition a wealth of dear associations. But, putting Mr. Lanier upon trial as an artist, it is fair to remember that probably none of these poems would have been republished by him without material alterations, the slightest of which no other hand can be authorized to make.

THE JACQUERIE—A FRAGMENT.

CHAPTER I.

ONCE on a time, a Dawn, all red and bright
Leapt on the conquered ramparts of the Night,
And flamed, one brilliant instant, on the world,
Then back into the historic moat was hurled
And Night was King again, for many years.
—Once on a time the Rose of Spring blushed out
But Winter angrily withdrew it back
Into his rough new-bursten husk, and shut
The stern husk-leaves, and hid it many years.
—Once Famine tricked himself with ears of corn,
And Hate strung flowers on his spikèd belt,
And glum Revenge in silver lilies pranked him,
And Lust put violets on his shameless front,
And all minced forth o' the street like holiday folk
That sally off afield on Summer morns.
—Once certain hounds that knew of many a chase,
And bare great wounds of antler and of tusk
That they had ta'en to give a lord some sport,
—Good hounds, that would have died to give lords sport—
Were so bewrayed and kicked by these same lords
That all the pack turned tooth o' the knights and bit
As knights had been no better things than boars,
And took revenge as bloody as a man's,
Unhoundlike, sudden, hot i' the chops, and sweet.
—Once sat a falcon on a lady's wrist,
Seeming to doze, with wrinkled eye-lid drawn,
But dreaming hard of hoods and slaveries
And of dim hungers in his heart and wings.

Then, while the mistress gazed above for game,
Sudden he flew into her painted face
And hooked his horn-claws in her lily throat
And drove his beak into her lips and eyes
In fierce and hawkish kissing that did scar
And mar the lady's beauty evermore.
—And once while Chivalry stood tall and lithe
And flashed his sword above the stricken eyes
Of all the simple peasant-folk of France :
While Thought was keen and hot and quick,
And did not play, as in these later days,
Like summer-lightning flickering in the west
—As little dreadful as if glow-worms lay
In the cool and watery clouds and glimmered weak—
But gleamed and struck at once or oak or man,
And left not space for Time to wave his wing
Betwixt the instantaneous flash and stroke :
While yet the needs of life were brave and fierce
And did not hide their deeds behind their words,
And logic came not 'twixt desire and act,
And Want-and-Take was the whole Form of life :
While Love had fires a-burning in his veins,
And hidden Hate could flash into revenge :
Ere yet young Trade was 'ware of his big thews
Or dreamed that in the bolder afterdays
He would hew down and bind old Chivalry
And drag him to the highest height of fame
And plunge him thence in the sea of still Romance
To lie for aye in never-rusted mail
Gleaming through quiet ripples of soft songs
And sheens of old traditionary tales :—
On such a time, a certain May arose
From out that blue Sea that between five lands
Lies like a violet midst of five large leaves,
Arose from out this violet and flew on

And stirred the spirits of the woods of France
And smoothed the brows of moody Auvergne hills,
And wrought warm sea-tints into maidens' eyes,
And calmed the wordy air of market-towns
With faint suggestions blown from distant buds,
Until the land seemed a mere dream of land,
And, in this dream-field Life sat like a dove
And cooed across unto her dove-mate Death,
Brooding, pathetic, by a river, lone.
Oh, sharper tangs pierced through this perfumed May.
Strange aches sailed by with odors on the wind
As when we kneel in flowers that grow on graves
Of friends who died unworthy of our love.
King John of France was proving such an ache
In English prisons wide and fair and grand,
Whose long expanses of green park and chace
Did ape large liberty with such success
As smiles of irony ape smiles of love.
Down from the oaks of Hertford Castle park,
Double with warm rose-breaths of southern Spring
Came rumors, as if odors too had thorns,
Sharp rumors, how the three Estates of France,
Like old Three-headed Cerberus of Hell
Had set upon the Duke of Normandy,
Their rightful Regent, snarled in his great face,
Snapped jagged teeth in inch-breadth of his throat,
And blown such hot and savage breath upon him,
That he had tossed great sops of royalty
Unto the clamorous, three-mawed baying beast.
And was not further on his way withal,
And had but changed a snarl into a growl:
How Arnold de Cervolles had ta'en the track
That war had burned along the unhappy land,
Shouting, *since France is then too poor to pay
The soldiers that have bloody devoir done,*

And since needs must, pardie! a man must eat,
Arm, gentlemen! swords slice as well as knives!
And so had tempted stout men from the ranks,
And now was adding robbers' waste to war's,
Stealing the leavings of remorseless battle,
And making gaunter the gaunt bones of want :
How this Cervolles (called " Arch-priest " by the mass)
Through warm Provence had marched and menace made
Against Pope Innocent at Avignon,
And how the Pope nor ate nor drank nor slept,
Through godly fear concerning his red wines.
For if these knaves should sack his holy house
And all the blessed casks be knocked o' the head,
Horrendum! all his Holiness' drink to be
Profanely guzzled down the reeking throats
Of scoundrels, and inflame them on to seize
The massy coffers of the Church's gold,
And steal, mayhap, the carven silver shrine
And all the golden crucifixes ?   No!—
And so the holy father Pope made stir
And had sent forth a legate to Cervolles,
And treated with him, and made compromise,
And, last, had bidden all the Arch-priest's troop
To come and banquet with him in his house,
Where they did wassail high by night and day
And Father Pope sat at the board and carved
   Midst jokes that flowed full greasily,
And priest and soldier trolled good songs for mass,
And all the prayers the Priests made were, *pray, drink,*
And all the oaths the Soldiers swore were, *drink!*
Till Mirth sat like a jaunty postillon
Upon the back of Time and urged him on
With piquant spur, past chapel and past cross :
How Charles, King of Navarre, in long duress
By mandate of King John within the walls

Of Crêvacœur and then of strong Allères,
In faithful ward of Sir Tristan du Bois,
Was now escaped, had supped with Guy Kyrec,
Had now a pardon of the Regent Duke
By half compulsion of a Paris mob,
Had turned the people's love upon himself
By smooth harangues, and now was bold to claim
That France was not the Kingdom of King John,
But, By our Lady, his, by right and worth,
And so was plotting treason in the State,
And laughing at weak Charles of Normandy.
Nay, these had been like good news to the King,
Were any man but bold enough to tell
The King what [bitter] sayings men had made
And hawked augmenting up and down the land
Against the barons and great lords of France
That fled from English arrows at Poictiers.
Poictiers, Poictiers : this grain i' the eye of France
Had swelled it to a big and bloodshot ball
That looked with rage upon a world askew.
Poictiers' disgrace was now but two years old,
Yet so outrageous rank and full was grown
That France was wholly overspread with shade,
And bitter fruits lay on the untilled ground
That stank and bred so foul contagious smells
That not a nose in France but stood awry,
Nor boor that cried not *faugh !* upon the air.

CHAPTER II.

FRANCISCAN friar John de Rochetaillade
With gentle gesture lifted up his hand
And poised it high above the steady eyes
Of a great crowd that thronged the market-place
In fair Clermont to hear him prophesy.

Midst of the crowd old Gris Grillon, the maimed,
—A wretched wreck that fate had floated out
From the drear storm of battle at Poictiers.
A living man whose larger moiety
Was dead and buried on the battle-field—
A grisly trunk, without or arms or legs,
And scarred with hoof-cuts over cheek and brow,
Lay in his wicker-cradle, smiling.

                                        " Jacques,"
Quoth he, " My son, I would behold this priest
That is not fat, and loves not wine, and fasts,
And stills the folk with waving of his hand,
And threats the knights and thunders at the Pope.
Make way for Gris, ye who are whole of limb !
Set me on yonder ledge, that I may see."
Forthwith a dozen horny hands reached out
And lifted Gris Grillon upon the ledge,
Whereon he lay and overlooked the crowd,
And from the gray-grown hedges of his brows
Shot forth a glance against the friar's eye
That struck him like an arrow.

                                  Then the friar,
With voice as low as if a maiden hummed
Love-songs of Provence in a mild day-dream :
" And when he broke the second seal, I heard
The second beast say, Come and see.

                                     And then
Went out another horse, and he was red.
And unto him that sat thereon was given
To take the peace of earth away, and set
Men killing one another : and they gave
To him a mighty sword."

                                The friar paused
And pointed round the circle of sad eyes.
" There is no face of man or woman here

But showeth print of the hard hoof of war.
Ah, yonder leaneth limbless Gris Grillon.
Friends, Gris Grillon is France.

                    Good France ; my France,
Wilt never walk on glory's hills again ?
Wilt never work among thy vines again ?
Art footless and art handless evermore ?
—Thou felon, War, I do arraign thee now
Of mayhem of the four main limbs of France !
Thou old red criminal, stand forth ; I charge
—But O, I am too utter sorrowful
To urge large accusation now.

                     Nathless,
My work to-day, is still more grievous.   Hear !
The stains that war hath wrought upon the land
Show but as faint white flecks, if seen o' the side
Of those blood-covered images that stalk
Through yon cold chambers of the future, as
The prophet-mood, now stealing on my soul,
Reveals them, marching, marching, marching.   See !
There go the kings of France, in piteous file.
The deadly diamonds shining in their crowns
Do wound the foreheads of their Majesties
And glitter through a setting of blood-gouts
As if they smiled to think how men are slain
By the sharp facets of the gem of power,
And how the kings of men are slaves of stones.
But look !   The long procession of the kings
Wavers and stops ; the world is full of noise,
The ragged peoples storm the palaces,
They rave, they laugh, they thirst, they lap the stream
That trickles from the regal vestments down,
And, lapping, smack their heated chaps for more,
And ply their daggers for it, till the kings
All die and lie in a crooked sprawl of death,

Ungainly, foul, and stiff as any heap
Of villeins rotting on a battle-field.
    'T is true, that when these things have come to pass
Then never a king shall rule again in France,
For every villein shall be king in France :
And who hath lordship in him, whether born
In hedge or silken bed, shall be a lord :
And queens shall be as thick i' the land as wives,
And all the maids shall maids of honor be :
And high and low shall commune solemnly :
And stars and stones shall have free interview.
But woe is me, 'tis also piteous true
That ere this gracious time shall visit France,
Your graves, Beloved, shall be some centuries old,
And so your children's, and their children's graves
And many generations'.
                              Ye, O ye
Shall grieve, and ye shall grieve, and ye shall grieve.
Your Life shall bend and o'er his shuttle toil,
A weaver weaving at the loom of grief.
Your Life shall sweat 'twixt anvil and hot forge,
An armorer working at the sword of grief.
Your Life shall moil i' the ground, and plant his seed,
A farmer foisoning a huge crop of grief.
Your Life shall chaffer in the market-place,
A merchant trading in the goods of grief.
Your Life shall go to battle with his bow,
A soldier fighting in defence of grief.
By every rudder that divides the seas,
Tall Grief shall stand, the helmsman of the ship.
By every wain that jolts along the roads,
Stout Grief shall walk, the driver of the team.
Midst every herd of cattle on the hills,
Dull Grief shall lie, the herdsman of the drove.

Oh Grief shall grind your bread and play your lutes
And marry you and bury you.
                              —How else?
Who's here in France, can win her people's faith
And stand in front and lead the people on?
Where is the Church?
                              The Church is far too fat.
Not, mark, by robust swelling of the thews,
But puffed and flabby large with gross increase
Of wine-fat, plague-fat, dropsy-fat.
                              O shame,
Thou Pope that cheatest God at Avignon,
Thou that shouldst be the Father of the world
And Regent of it whilst our God is gone;
Thou that shouldst blaze with conferred majesty
And smite old Lust-o'-the-Flesh so as by flame;
Thou that canst turn thy key and lock Grief up
Or turn thy key and unlock Heaven's Gate,
Thou that shouldst be the veritable hand
That Christ down-stretcheth out of heaven yet
To draw up him that fainteth to His heart,
Thou that shouldst bear thy fruit, yet virgin live,
As she that bore a man yet sinnèd not,
Thou that shouldst challenge the most special eyes
Of Heaven and Earth and Hell to mark thee, since
Thou shouldst be Heaven's best captain, Earth's best friend,
And Hell's best enemy—false Pope, false Pope,
The world, thy child, is sick and like to die,
But thou art dinner-drowsy and cannot come:
And Life is sore beset and crieth *help!*
But thou brook'st not disturbance at thy wine:
And France is wild for one to lead her souls;
But thou art huge and fat and laggest back
Among the remnants of forsaken camps.
Thou 'rt not God's Pope, thou art the Devil's Pope.

Thou art first Squire to that most puissant knight,
Lord Satan, who thy faithful squireship long
Hath watched and well shall guerdon.

                           Ye sad souls,
So faint with work ye love not, so thin-worn
With miseries ye wrought not, so outraged
By strokes of ill that pass th' ill-doers' heads
And cleave the innocent, so desperate tired
Of insult that doth day by day abuse
The humblest dignity of humblest men,
Ye cannot call toward the Church for help.
The Church already is o'erworked with care
Of its dyspeptic stomach.

                      Ha, the Church
Forgets about eternity.

                  I had
A vision of forgetfulness.

               O Dream
Born of a dream, as yonder cloud is born
Of water which is born of cloud !

                    I thought
I saw the moonlight lying large and calm
Upon the unthrobbing bosom of the earth,
As a great diamond glittering on a shroud.
A sense of breathlessness stilled all the world.
Motion stood dreaming he was changed to Rest,
And Life asleep did fancy he was Death.
A quick small shadow spotted the white world ;
Then instantly 'twas huge, and huger grew
By instants till it did o'ergloom all space.
I lifted up mine eyes—O thou just God !
I saw a spectre with a million heads
Come frantic downward through the universe,
And all the mouths of it were uttering cries,
Wherein was a sharp agony, and yet

The cries were much like laughs : as if Pain laugned.
Its myriad lips were blue, and sometimes they
Closed fast and only moaned dim sounds that shaped
Themselves to one word, *Homeless*, and the stars
Did utter back the moan, and the great hills
Did bellow it, and then the stars and hills
Bandied the grief o' the ghost 'twixt heaven and earth.
The spectre sank, and lay upon the air,
And brooded, level, close upon the earth,
With all the myriad heads just over me.
I glanced in all the eyes and marked that some
Did glitter with a flame of lunacy,
And some were soft and false as feigning love,
And some were blinking with hypocrisy,
And some were overfilmed by sense, and some
Blazed with ambition's wild, unsteady fire,
And some were burnt i' the sockets black, and some
Were dead as embers when the fire is out.
A curious zone circled the Spectre's waist,
Which seemed with strange device to symbol Time.
It was a silver-gleaming thread of day
Spiral about a jet-black band of night.
This zone seemed ever to contract and all
The frame with momentary spasms heaved
In the strangling traction which did never cease.
I cried unto the spectre, *Time hath bound
Thy body with the fibre of his hours.*
Then rose a multitude of mocking sounds,
And some mouths spat at me and cried *thou fool*,
And some, *thou liest*, and some, *he dreams :* and then
Some hands uplifted certain bowls they bore
To lips that writhed but drank with eagerness.
And some played curious viols, shaped like hearts
And stringed with loves, to light and ribald tunes,
　　And other hands slit throats with knives,

9

And others patted all the painted cheeks
In reach, and others stole what others had
Unseen, or boldly snatched at alien rights,
And some o' the heads did vie in a foolish game
Of which could hold itself the highest, and
Of which one's neck was stiff the longest time.

  And then the sea in silence wove a veil
Of mist, and breathed it upward and about,
And waved and wound it softly round the world,
And meshed my dream i' the vague and endless folds,
And a light wind arose and blew these off,
And I awoke.

                      The many heads are priests
That have forgot eternity : and Time
  Hath caught and bound them with a withe
Into a fagot huge, to burn in hell.
—Now if the priesthood put such shame upon
Your cry for leadership, can better help
Come out of knighthood ?

                          Lo ! you smile, you boors ?
You villeins smile at knighthood ?

                              Now, thou France
That wert the mother of fair chivalry,
Unclose thine eyes, unclose thine eyes, here, see,
Here stand a herd of knaves that laugh to scorn
Thy gentlemen !

                    O contumely hard,
O bitterness of last disgrace, O sting
That stings the coward knights of lost Poictiers !
I would—" but now a murmur rose i' the crowd
Of angry voices, and the friar leapt
From where he stood to preach and pressed a path
Betwixt the mass that way the voices came.

CHAPTER III.

LORD RAOUL was riding castleward from field.
At left hand rode his lady and at right
His fool whom he loved better; and his bird,
His fine ger-falcon best beloved of all,
Sat hooded on his wrist and gently swayed
To the undulating amble of the horse.
Guest-knights and huntsmen and a noisy train
Of loyal-stomached flatterers and their squires
Clattered in retinue, and aped his pace,
And timed their talk by his, and worked their eyes
By intimation of his glance, with great
And drilled precision.
                            Then said the fool:
" 'Twas a brave flight, my lord, that last one ! brave.
Didst note the heron once did turn about,
And show a certain anger with his wing,
And make as if he almost dared, not quite,
To strike the falcon, ere the falcon him?
A foolish damnable advisèd bird,
Yon heron ! What? Shall herons grapple hawks?
God made the herons for the hawks to strike,
And hawk and heron made he for lords' sport."
" What then, my honey-tonguèd Fool, that knowest
God's purposes, what made he fools for?"
                                            " For
To counsel lords, my lord. Wilt hear me prove
Fools' counsel better than wise men's advice?"
" Aye, prove it. If thy logic fail, wise fool,
I'll cause two wise men whip thee soundly."
                                            " So:

Wise men are prudent : prudent men have care
For their own proper interest ; therefore they

Advise their own advantage, not another's.
But fools are careless : careless men care not
For their own proper interest ; therefore they
Advise their friend's advantage, not their own.
Now hear the commentary, Cousin Raoul.
This fool, unselfish, counsels thee, his lord,
Go not through yonder square, where, as thou see'st
Yon herd of villeins, crick-necked all with strain
Of gazing upward, stand, and gaze, and take
With open mouth and eye and ear, the quips
And heresies of John de Rochetaillade."
Lord Raoul half turned him in his saddle round,
And looked upon his fool and vouchsafed him
What moiety of fastidious wonderment
A generous nobleness could deign to give
To such humility, with eye superb
Where languor and surprise both showed themselves,
Each deprecating t'other.

                " Now, dear knave,
Be kind and tell me—tell me quickly, too,—
Some proper reasonable ground or cause,
Nay, tell me but some shadow of some cause,
Nay, hint me but a thin ghost's dream of cause,
(So will I thee absolve from being whipped)
Why I, Lord Raoul, should turn my horse aside
From riding by yon pitiful villein gang,
Or ay, by God, from riding o'er their heads
If so my humor serve, or through their bodies,
Or miring fetlocks in their nasty brains,
Or doing aught else I will in my Clermont?
Do me this grace, mine Idiot."

                  " Please thy Wisdom
An thou dost ride through this same gang of boors,
'Tis my fool's-prophecy, some ill shall fall.
Lord Raoul, yon mass of various flesh is fused

And melted quite in one by white-hot words
The friar speaks.   Sir, sawest thou ne'er, sometimes,
Thine armorer spit on iron when 'twas hot,
And how the iron flung the insult back,
Hissing?   So this contempt now in thine eye,
If it shall fall on yonder heated surface
May bounce back upward.   Well : and then?   What then?
Why, if thou cause thy folk to crop some villein's ears,
So, evil falls, and a fool foretells the truth.
Or if some erring crossbow-bolt should break
Thine unarmed head, shot from behind a house,
So, evil falls, and a fool foretells the truth."
" Well," quoth Lord Raoul, with languid utterance,
" 'Tis very well—and thou 'rt a foolish fool,
Nay, thou art Folly's perfect witless man,
Stupidity doth madly dote on thee,
And Idiocy doth fight her for thy love,
Yet Silliness doth love thee best of all,
And while they quarrel, snatcheth thee to her
And saith *Ah ! 'tis my sweetest No-brains : mine !*
—And 'tis my mood to-day some ill shall fall."
And there right suddenly Lord Raoul gave rein
And galloped straightway to the crowded square,
—What time a strange light flickered in the eyes
Of the calm fool, that was not folly's gleam,
But more like wisdom's smile at plan well laid
And end well compassed.   In the noise of hoofs
Secure, the fool low-muttered : " *Folly's love!*
So : *Silliness' sweetheart : no-brains :* quoth my Lord.
Why, how intolerable an ass is he
Whom Silliness' sweetheart drives so, by the ear !
Thou languid, lordly, most heart-breaking Nought !
Thou bastard zero, that hast come to power,
Nothing's right issue failing !   Thou mere ' pooh '
That Life hath uttered in some moment's pet,

And then forgot she uttered thee ! Thou gap
In time, thou little notch in circumstance ! "

CHAPTER IV.

LORD RAOUL drew rein with all his company,
And urged his horse i' the crowd, to gain fair view
Of him that spoke, and stopped at last, and sat
Still, underneath where Gris Grillon was laid,
And heard, somewhile, with languid scornful gaze,
The friar putting blame on priest and knight.
But presently, as 'twere in weariness,
He gazed about, and then above, and so
Made mark of Gris Grillon.

     " So, there, old man,
Thou hast more brows than legs ! "

       " I would," quoth Gris,
" That thou, upon a certain time I wot,
Hadst had less legs and bigger brows, my Lord ! "
Then all the flatterers and their squires cried out
Solicitous, with various voice, " Go to,
Old Rogue," or " Shall I brain him, my good Lord ? "
Or, " So, let me but chuck him from his perch,"
Or, "Slice his tongue to piece his leg withal,"
Or, " Send his eyes to look for his missing arms."
But my Lord Raoul was in the mood, to-day,
Which craves suggestions simply with a view
To flout them in the face, and so waved hand
Backward, and stayed the on-pressing sycophants
Eager to buy rich praise with bravery cheap.
"I would know why,"—he said—" thou wishedst me
Less legs and bigger brows ; and when ? "

       " Wouldst know?
Learn then," cried Gris Grillon and stirred himself,
In a great spasm of passion mixed with pain ;

" An thou hadst had more courage and less speed,
Then, ah my God ! then could not I have been
That piteous gibe of a man thou see 'st I am.
Sir, having no disease, nor any taint
Nor old hereditament of sin or shame,
—But, feeling the brave bound and energy
Of daring health that leaps along the veins—
As a hart upon his river banks at morn,
—Sir, wild with the urgings and hot strenuous beats
Of manhood's heart in this full-sinewed breast
Which thou may'st even now discern is mine,
—Sir, full aware, each instant in each day,
Of motions of great muscles, once were mine,
And thrill of tense thew-knots, and stinging sense
Of nerves, nice, capable and delicate :
—Sir, visited each hour by passions great
That lack all instrument of utterance,
Passion of love—that hath no arm to curve ;
Passion of speed—that hath no limb to stretch ;
Yea, even that poor feeling of desire
Simply to turn me from this side to that,
(Which brooded on, into wild passion grows
By reason of the impotence that broods)
Balked of its end and unachievable
Without assistance of some foreign arm,
—Sir, moved and thrilled like any perfect man,
O, trebly moved and thrilled, since poor desires
That are of small import to happy men
Who easily can compass them, to me
Become mere hopeless Heavens or actual Hells,
—Sir, strengthened so with manhood's seasoned soul,
I lie in this damned cradle day and night,
Still, still, so still, my Lord : less than a babe
In powers but more than any man in needs ;
Dreaming, with open eye, of days when men

Have fallen cloven through steel and bone and flesh
At single strokes of this—of that big arm
Once wielded aught a mortal arm might wield,
Waking a prey to any foolish gnat
That wills to conquer my defenceless brow
And sit thereon in triumph ; hounded ever
By small necessities of barest use
Which, since I cannot compass them alone,
Do snarl my helplessness into mine ear,
Howling behind me that I have no hands,
And yelping round me that I have no feet :
So that my heart is stretched by tiny ills
That are so much the larger that I knew
In bygone days how trifling small they were :
—Dungeoned in wicker, strong as 'twere in stone ;
—Fast chained with nothing, firmer than with steel ;
—Captive in limb, yet free in eye and ear,
Sole tenant of this puny Hell in Heaven :
—And this—all this—because I was a man !
For, in the battle—ha, thou know'st, pale-face !
When that the four great English horsemen bore
So bloodily on thee, I leapt to front
To front of thee—of thee—and fought four blades,
Thinking to win thee time to snatch thy breath,
And, by a rearing fore-hoof stricken down,
  Mine eyes, through blood, my brain, through pain,
—Midst of a dim hot uproar fainting down—
Were 'ware of thee, far rearward, fleeing ! Hound !"

CHAPTER V.

THEN, as the passion of old Gris Grillon
A wave swift swelling, grew to highest height
And snapped a foaming consummation forth
With salty hissing, came the friar through

The mass.   A stillness of white faces wrought
A transient death on all the hands and breasts
Of all the crowd, and men and women stood,
One instant, fixed, as they had died upright.
Then suddenly Lord Raoul rose up in selle
And thrust his dagger straight upon the breast
Of Gris Grillon, to pin him to the wall ;
But ere steel-point met flesh, tall Jacques Grillon
Had leapt straight upward from the earth, and in
The self-same act had whirled his bow by end
With mighty whirr about his head, and struck
The dagger with so featly stroke and full
That blade flew up and hilt flew down, and left
Lord Raoul unfriended of his weapon.
                                                      Then
The fool cried shrilly, " Shall a knight of France
Go stabbing his own cattle ?"   And Lord Raoul,
Calm with a changing mood, sat still and called :
" Here, huntsmen, 'tis my will ye seize the hind
That broke my dagger, bind him to this tree
And slice both ears to hair-breadth of his head,
To be his bloody token of regret
That he hath put them to so foul employ
As catching villainous breath of strolling priests
That mouth at knighthood and defile the Church."
The knife   .   .   .   .   .   [Rest of line lost.]
To place the edge   .   .   .   .   [Rest of line lost.]
Mary ! the blood ! it oozes sluggishly,
Scorning to come at call of blade so base.
Sathanas !   He that cuts the ear has left
The blade sticking at midway, for to turn
   And ask the Duke " if 'tis not done
Thus far with nice precision," and the Duke
Leans down to see, and cries, " 'tis marvellous nice,
Shaved as thou wert ear-barber by profession ! "
   9*

Whereat one witling cries, " 'tis monstrous fit,
In sooth, a shaven-pated priest should have
A shaven-earèd audience ; " and another,
"Give thanks, thou Jacques, to this most gracious Duke
That rids thee of the life-long dread of loss
Of thy two ears, by cropping them at once ;
And now henceforth full safely thou may'st dare
The powerfullest Lord in France to touch
An ear of thine ; " and now the knave o' the knife
Seizes the handle to commence again, and saws
And . . ha! Lift up thine head, O Henry! Friend!
'Tis Marie, walking midway of the street,
As she had just stepped forth from out the gate
Of the very, very Heaven where God is,
Still glittering with the God-shine on her! Look!
And there right suddenly the fool looked up
And saw the crowd divided in two ranks.
Raoul pale-stricken as a man that waits
God's first remark when he hath died into
God's sudden presence, saw the cropping knave
A-pause with knife in hand, the wondering folk
All straining forward with round-ringèd eyes,
And Gris Grillon calm smiling while he prayed
The Holy Virgin's blessing.
                                        Down the lane
Betwixt the hedging bodies of the crowd,
[Part of line lost.]   .   .   .   .   majesty
[Part of line lost.]   .   .   a spirit pacing on the top
Of springy clouds, and bore straight on toward
The Duke. On him her eyes burned steadily
With such gray fires of heaven-hot command
As Dawn burns Night away with, and she held
Her white forefinger quivering aloft
At greatest arm's-length of her dainty arm,
In menace sweeter than a kiss could be

And terribler than sudden whispers are
That come from lips unseen, in sunlit room.
So with the spell of all the Powers of Sense
That e'er have swayed the savagery of hot blood
Raying from her whole body beautiful,
She held the eyes and wills of all the crowd.
Then from the numbèd hand of him that cut,
The knife dropped down, and the quick fool stole in
And snatched and deftly severed all the withes
Unseen, and Jacques burst forth into the crowd,
And then the mass completed the long breath
They had forgot to draw, and surged upon
The centre where the maiden stood with sound
Of multitudes of blessings, and Lord Raoul
Rode homeward, silent and most pale and strange,
Deep-wrapt in moody fits of hot and cold.

(End of Chapter V.)

.   .   .   .

Macon, Georgia, 1868.

SONG FOR "THE JACQUERIE."

MAY the maiden,
Violet-laden
Out of the violet sea,
Comes and hovers
Over lovers,
Over thee, Marie, and me,
Over me and thee.

Day the stately,
Sunken lately
Into the violet sea,
Backward hovers
Over lovers,
Over thee, Marie, and me,
Over me and thee.

Night the holy,
Sailing slowly
Over the violet sea,
Stars uncovers
Over lovers,
Stars for thee, Marie, and me,
Stars for me and thee.

MACON, GEORGIA, 1868.

SONG FOR "THE JACQUERIE."

BETRAYAL.

THE sun has kissed the violet sea,
  And burned the violet to a rose.
O Sea! wouldst thou not better be
  Mere violet still ?   Who knows ? who knows ?
      Well hides the violet in the wood :
      The dead leaf wrinkles her a hood,
      And winter's ill is violet's good ;
      But the bold glory of the rose,
      It quickly comes and quickly goes—
      Red petals whirling in white snows,
          Ah me !

The sun has burnt the rose-red sea :
  The rose is turned to ashes gray.
O Sea, O Sea, mightst thou but be
  The violet thou hast been to-day !
      The sun is brave, the sun is bright,
      The sun is lord of love and light ;
      But after him it cometh night.
      Dim anguish of the lonesome dark !—
      Once a girl's body, stiff and stark,
      Was laid in a tomb without a mark,
          Ah me !

MACON, GEORGIA, 1868.

SONG FOR "THE JACQUERIE."

THE hound was cuffed, the hound was kicked,
O' the ears was cropped, o' the tail was nicked,
(*All.*)   Oo-hoo-o, howled the hound.
The hound into his kennel crept ;
He rarely wept, he never slept.
His mouth he always open kept
    Licking his bitter wound,
      The hound,
(*All.*)   U-lu-lo, *howled the hound.*

A star upon his kennel shone
That showed the hound a meat-bare bone.
(*All.*)   O hungry was the hound !
The hound had but a churlish wit.
He seized the bone, he crunched, he bit.
" An thou wert Master, I had slit
    Thy throat with a huge wound,"
      Quo' hound.
(*All.*)   O, angry was the hound.

The star in castle-window shone,
The Master lay abed, alone.
(*All.*)   Oh ho, why not ? quo' hound.
He leapt, he seized the throat, he tore
The Master, head from neck, to floor,
And rolled the head i' the kennel door,
    And fled and salved his wound,
      Good hound !
(*All.*)   U-lu-lo, *howled the hound.*

MACON, GEORGIA, 1868.

THE GOLDEN WEDDING OF STERLING AND SARAH LANIER,

SEPTEMBER 27, 1868.

BY THE ELDEST GRANDSON.

A RAINBOW span of fifty years,
Painted upon a cloud of tears,
In blue for hopes and red for fears,
    Finds end in a golden hour to-day.
Ah, *you* to our childhood the legend told,
" At the end of the rainbow lies the gold,"
And now in our thrilling hearts we hold
    The gold that never will pass away.

Gold crushed from the quartz of a crystal life,
Gold hammered with blows of human strife,
Gold burnt in the love of man and wife,
    Till it is pure as the very flame :
Gold that the miser will not have,
Gold that is good beyond the grave,
Gold that the patient and the brave
    Amass, neglecting praise and blame.

O golden hour that caps the time
Since, heart to heart like rhyme to rhyme,
You stood and listened to the chime
    Of inner bells by spirits rung,
That tinkled many a secret sweet
Concerning how two souls should meet,
And whispered of Time's flying feet
    With a most piquant silver tongue.

O golden day,—a golden crown
For the kingly heads that bowed not down
To win a smile or 'scape a frown,
 Except the smile and frown of Heaven!
Dear heads, still dark with raven hair;
Dear hearts, still white in spite of care;
Dear eyes, still black and bright and fair
 As any eyes to mortals given!

Old parents of a restless race,
You miss full many a bonny face
That would have smiled a filial grace
 Around your Golden Wedding wine.
But God is good and God is great.
His will be done, if soon or late.
Your dead stand happy in yon Gate
 And call you blessed while they shine.

So, drop the tear and dry the eyes.
Your rainbow glitters in the skies.
Here's golden wine: young, old, arise:
 With cups as full as our souls, we say:
" Two Hearts, that wrought with smiles through tears
This rainbow span of fifty years,
Behold how true, true love appears
 True gold for your Golden Wedding day! "

MACON, GEORGIA, September, 1868.

STRANGE JOKES.

WELL : Death is a huge omnivorous Toad
Grim squatting on a twilight road.
He catcheth all that Circumstance
  Hath tossed to him.
He curseth all who upward glance
  As lost to him.

Once in a whimsey mood he sat
And talked of life, in proverbs pat,
To Eve in Eden,—" Death, on Life "—
  As if he knew !
And so he toadied Adam's wife
  There, in the dew.

O dainty dew, O morning dew
That gleamed in the world's first dawn, did you
And the sweet grass and manful oaks
  Give lair and rest
To him who toadwise sits and croaks
  His death-behest?

Who fears the hungry Toad ?   Not I !
He but unfetters me to fly.
The German still, when one is dead,
  Cries out " Der Tod ! "
But, pilgrims, Christ will walk ahead
  And clear the road.

MACON, GEORGIA, July, 1867.

NIRVANA.

THROUGH seas of dreams and seas of phantasies,
Through seas of solitudes and vacancies,
And through my Self, the deepest of the seas,
    I strive to thee, Nirvâna.

Oh long ago the billow-flow of sense,
Aroused by passion's windy vehemence,
Upbore me out of depths to heights intense,
    But not to thee, Nirvâna.

By waves swept on, I learned to ride the waves.
I served my masters till I made them slaves.
I baffled Death by hiding in his graves,
    His watery graves, Nirvâna.

And once I clomb a mountain's stony crown
And stood, and smiled no smile and frowned no frown,
Nor ate, nor drank, nor slept, nor faltered down,
    Five days and nights, Nirvana.

Sunrise and noon and sunset and strange night
And shadow of large clouds and faint starlight
And lonesome Terror stalking round the height,
    I minded not, Nirvâna.

The silence ground my soul keen like a spear.
My bare thought, whetted as a sword, cut sheer
Through time and life and flesh and death, to clear
    My way unto Nirvâna.

I slew gross bodies of old ethnic hates
That stirred long race-wars betwixt States and States.
I stood and scorned these foolish dead debates,
    Calmly, calmly, Nirvâna.

I smote away the filmy base of Caste.
I thrust through antique blood and riches vast,
And all big claims of the pretentious Past
    That hindered my Nirvâna.

Then all fair types, of form and sound and hue,
Up-floated round my sense and charmed anew.
—I waved them back into the void blue :
    I love them not, Nirvâna.

And all outrageous ugliness of time,
Excess and Blasphemy and squinting Crime
Beset me, but I kept my calm sublime :
    I hate them not, Nirvâna.

High on the topmost thrilling of the surge
I saw, afar, two hosts to battle urge.
The widows of the victors sang a dirge,
    But I wept not, Nirvâna.

I saw two lovers sitting on a star.
He kissed her lip, she kissed his battle-scar.
They quarrelled soon, and went two ways, afar.
    O Life ! I laughed, Nirvâna.

And never a king but had some king above,
And never a law to right the wrongs of Love,
And ever a fangèd snake beneath a dove,
    Saw I on earth, Nirvâna.

But I, with kingship over kings, am free.
I love not, hate not : right and wrong agree :
And fangs of snakes and lures of doves to me
      Are vain, are vain, Nirvâna.

So by mine inner contemplation long,
By thoughts that need no speech nor oath nor song,
My spirit soars above the motley throng
      Of days and nights, Nirvâna.

O Suns, O Rains, O Day and Night, O Chance,
O Time besprent with seven-hued circumstance,
I float above ye all into the trance
      That draws me nigh Nirvâna.

Gods of small worlds, ye little Deities
Of humble Heavens under my large skies,
And Governor-Spirits, all, I rise, I rise,
      I rise into Nirvâna.

The storms of Self below me rage and die.
On the still bosom of mine ecstasy,
A lotus on a lake of balm, I lie
      Forever in Nirvâna.

MACON, GEORGIA, 1869.

THE RAVEN DAYS.

OUR hearths are gone out and our hearts are broken,
   And but the ghosts of homes to us remain,
And ghastly eyes and hollow sighs give token
   From friend to friend of an unspoken pain.

O Raven days, dark Raven days of sorrow,
   Bring to us in your whetted ivory beaks
Some sign out of the far land of To-morrow,
   Some strip of sea-green dawn, some orange streaks.

Ye float in dusky files, forever croaking.
   Ye chill our manhood with your dreary shade.
Dumb in the dark, not even God invoking,
   We lie in chains, too weak to be afraid.

O Raven days, dark Raven days of sorrow,
   Will ever any warm light come again?
Will ever the lit mountains of To-morrow
   Begin to gleam athwart the mournful plain?

PRATTVILLE, ALABAMA, February, 1868.

---

[1] The two poems which follow "The Raven Days" have not been included in earlier editions. All three are calls from those desperate years for the South just after the Civil War. The reader of to-day, seeing that forlorn period in the just perspective of half a century, will not wonder at the tone of anguished remonstrance; but, rather, that so few notes of mourning have come from a poet who missed nothing of what the days of Reconstruction brought to his people.

OUR HILLS.

DEAR Mother-Earth
Of Titan birth,
Yon hills are your large breasts, and often I
Have climbed to their top-nipples, fain and dry
To drink my mother's-milk so near the sky.

O ye hill-stains,
Red, for all rains!
The blood that made you has all bled for us,
The hearts that paid you are all dead for us,
The trees that shade you groan with lead, for us!

And O, hill-sides,
Like giants' brides
Ye sleep in ravine-rumpled draperies,
And weep your springs in tearful memories
Of days that stained your robes with stains like these!

Sleep on, ye hills!
Weep on, ye rills!
The stainers have decreed the stains shall stay.
They chain the hands might wash the stains away.
They wait with cold hearts till we "rue the day."

O Mother-Earth
Of Titan birth,
Thy mother's-milk is curdled with aloe.
—Like hills, Men, lift calm heads through any woe,
And weep, but bow not an inch, for any foe!

Thou Sorrow-height
We climb by night,
Thou hast no hell-deep chasm save Disgrace.
To stoop, will fling us down its foulèd space:
Stand proud! The Dawn will meet us, face to face,
For down steep hills the Dawn loves best to race!

LAUGHTER IN THE SENATE.

In the South lies a lonesome, hungry Land;
He huddles his rags with a cripple's hand;
He mutters, prone on the barren sand,
              What time his heart is breaking.

He lifts his bare head from the ground;
He listens through the gloom around:
The winds have brought him a strange sound
              Of distant merrymaking.

Comes now the Peace so long delayed?
Is it the cheerful voice of Aid?
Begins the time his heart has prayed,
              When men may reap and sow?

Ah, God! Back to the cold earth's breast!
The sages chuckle o'er their jest;
Must they, to give a people rest,
              Their dainty wit forego?

The tyrants sit in a stately hall;
They jibe at a wretched people's fall;
The tyrants forget how fresh is the pall
              Over their dead and ours.

Look how the senators ape the clown,
And don the motley and hide the gown,
But yonder a fast-rising frown
              On the people's forehead lowers.

1868.

BABY CHARLEY.

HE 's fast asleep.   See how, O Wife,
Night's finger on the lip of life
Bids whist the tongue, so prattle-rife,
    Of busy Baby Charley.

One arm stretched backward round his head,
Five little toes from out the bed
Just showing, like five rosebuds red,
    —So slumbers Baby Charley.

Heaven-lights, I know, are beaming through
Those lucent eyelids, veined with blue,
That shut away from mortal view
    Large eyes of Baby Charley.

O **sweet**.Sleep-Angel, throned now
On the round glory of his brow,
Wave thy wing and waft my vow
    Breathed over Baby Charley.

I vow that my heart, when death is nigh,
Shall never shiver with a sigh
For act of hand or tongue or eye
    That wronged my Baby Charley!

MACON, GEORGIA, December, 1869.

A SEA-SHORE GRAVE.

To M. J. L.

BY SIDNEY AND CLIFFORD LANIER.

O WISH that's vainer than the plash
    Of these wave-whimsies on the shore :
" Give us a pearl to fill the gash—
    God, let our dead friend live once more ! "

O wish that's stronger than the stroke
    Of yelling wave and snapping levin ;
" God, lift us o'er the Last Day's smoke,
    All white, to Thee and her in Heaven ! "

O wish that's swifter than the race
    Of wave and wind in sea and sky ;
Let's take the grave-cloth from her face
    And fall in the grave, and kiss, and die !

Look ! High above a glittering calm
    Of sea and sky and kingly sun,
She shines and smiles, and waves a palm—
    And now we wish—Thy will be done !

MONTGOMERY, ALABAMA, 1866.

SOULS AND RAIN-DROPS.

LIGHT rain-drops fall and wrinkle the sea,
Then vanish, and die utterly.
One would not know that rain-drops fell
If the round sea-wrinkles did not tell.

So souls come down and wrinkle life
And vanish in the flesh-sea strife.
One might not know that souls had place
Were 't not for the wrinkles in life's face.

NILSSON.

A ROSE of perfect red, embossed
With silver sheens of crystal frost,
Yet warm, nor life nor fragrance lost.

High passion throbbing in a sphere
That Art hath wrought of diamond clear,
—A great heart beating in a tear.

The listening soul is full of dreams
That shape the wondrous-varying themes
As cries of men or plash of streams.

Or noise of summer rain-drops round
That patter daintily a-ground
With hints of heaven in the sound.

Or noble wind-tones chanting free
Through morning-skies across the sea
Wild hymns to some strange majesty.

O, if one trope, clear-cut and keen,
May type the art of Song's best queen,
White-hot of soul, white-chaste of mien,

On Music's heart doth Nilsson dwell
As if a Swedish snow-flake fell
Into a glowing flower-bell.

NEW YORK, 1871.

10

NIGHT AND DAY.

THE innocent, sweet Day is dead.
Dark Night hath slain her in her bed.
O, Moors are as fierce to kill as to wed !
  —Put out the light, said he.

A sweeter light than ever rayed
From star of heaven or eye of maid
Has vanished in the unknown Shade.
  —She 's dead, she 's dead, said he.

Now, in a wild, sad after-mood
The tawny Night sits still to brood
Upon the dawn-time when he wooed.
  —I would she lived, said he.

Star-memories of happier times,
Of loving deeds and lovers' rhymes,
Throng forth in silvery pantomimes.
  —Come back, O Day ! said he.

MONTGOMERY, ALABAMA, 1866.

A BIRTHDAY SONG.

To S. G.

FOR ever wave, for ever float and shine
Before my yearning eyes, oh! dream of mine
Wherein I dreamed that time was like a vine,

A creeping rose, that clomb a height of dread
Out of the sea of Birth, all filled with dead,
Up to the brilliant cloud of Death o'erhead.

This vine bore many blossoms, which were years.
Their petals, red with joy, or bleached by tears,
Waved to and fro i' the winds of hopes and fears.

Here all men clung, each hanging by his spray.
Anon, one dropped; his neighbor 'gan to pray;
And so they clung and dropped and prayed, alway.

But I did mark one lately-opened bloom,
Wherefrom arose a visible perfume
That wrapped me in a cloud of dainty gloom.

And rose—an odor by a spirit haunted—
And drew me upward with a speed enchanted,
Swift floating, by wild sea or sky undaunted,

Straight through the cloud of death, where men are free.
I gained a height, and stayed and bent my knee.
Then glowed my cloud, and broke and unveiled thee.

" O flower-born and flower-souled!" I said,
" Be the year-bloom that breathed thee ever red,
 Nor wither, yellow, down among the dead.

" May all that cling to sprays of time, like me,
 Be sweetly wafted over sky and sea
 By rose-breaths shrining maidens like to thee!"

Then while we sat upon the height afar
Came twilight, like a lover late from war,
With soft winds fluting to his evening star.

And the shy stars grew bold and scattered gold,
And chanting voices ancient secrets told,
And an acclaim of angels earthward rolled.

MONTGOMERY, ALABAMA, October, 1866.

RESURRECTION.

SOMETIMES in morning sunlights by the river
   Where in the early fall long grasses wave,
Light winds from over the moorland sink and shiver
   And sigh as if just blown across a grave.

And then I pause and listen to this sighing.
   I look with strange eyes on the well-known stream.
I hear wild birth-cries uttered by the dying.
   I know men waking who appear to dream.

Then from the water-lilies slow uprises
   The still vast face of all the life I know,
Changed now, and full of wonders and surprises,
   With fire in eyes that once were glazed with snow.

Fair now the brows old Pain had erewhile wrinkled,
   And peace and strength about the calm mouth dwell.
Clean of the ashes that Repentance sprinkled,
   The meek head poises like a flower-bell.

All the old scars of wanton wars are vanished ;
   And what blue bruises grappling Sense had left
And sad remains of redder stains are banished,
   And the dim blotch of heart-committed theft.

O still vast vision of transfigured features
   Unvisited by secret crimes or dooms,
Remain, remain amid these water-creatures,
   Stand, shine among yon water-lily blooms.

For eighteen centuries ripple down the river,
   And windy times the stalks of empires wave,
—Let the winds come from the moor and sigh and shiver,
   Fain, fain am I, O Christ, to pass the grave.

TO ——.

THE Day was dying ; his breath
Wavered away in a hectic gleam ;
And I said, if Life 's a dream, and Death
And Love and all are dreams—I 'll dream.

A mist came over the bay
Like as a dream would over an eye.
The mist was white and the dream was grey
And both contained a human cry,

The burthen whereof was " Love,"
And it filled both mist and dream with pain,
And the hills below and the skies above
Were touched and uttered it back again.

The mist broke : down the rift
A kind ray shot from a holy star.
Then my dream did waver and break and lift—
Through it, O Love, shone thy face, afar.

So Boyhood sets : comes Youth,
A painful night of mists and dreams ;
That broods till Love's exquisite truth,
The star of a morn-clear manhood, beams.

BOYKIN'S BLUFF, VIRGINIA, 1863.

THE WEDDING.

O MARRIAGE-BELLS, your clamor tells
  Two weddings in one breath.
She marries whom her love compels :
  —And I wed Goodman Death !
My brain is blank, my tears are red ;
Listen, O God :—" I will," he said :—
And I would that I were dead.
Come groomsman Grief and bridesmaid Pain
Come and stand with a ghastly twain.
My Bridegroom Death is come o'er the meres
To wed a bride with bloody tears.
Ring, ring, O bells, full merrily :
Life-bells to her, death-bells to me :
O Death, I am true wife to thee !

MACON, GEORGIA, 1865.

THE PALM AND THE PINE.

FROM THE GERMAN OF HEINE.

In the far North stands a Pine-tree, lone,
   Upon a wintry height ;
It sleeps : around it snows have thrown
   A covering of white.

It dreams forever of a Palm
   That, far i' the Morning-land,
Stands silent in a most sad calm
   Midst of the burning sand.

Point Lookout Prison, 1864.

SPRING GREETING.

FROM THE GERMAN OF HERDER.

ALL faintly through my soul to-day,
As from a bell that far away
Is tinkled by some frolic fay,
    Floateth a lovely chiming.
Thou magic bell, to many a fell
And many a winter-saddened dell
Thy tongue a tale of Spring doth tell,
    Too passionate-sweet for rhyming.

Chime out, thou little song of Spring,
Float in the blue skies ravishing.
Thy song-of-life a joy doth bring
    That 's sweet, albeit fleeting.
Float on the Spring-winds e'en to my home :
And when thou to a rose shalt come
That hath begun to show her bloom,
    Say, I send her greeting!

POINT LOOKOUT PRISON, 1864.

THE TOURNAMENT.

JOUST FIRST.

I.

BRIGHT shone the lists, blue bent the skies,
  And the knights still hurried amain
To the tournament under the ladies' eyes,
  Where the jousters were Heart and Brain.

II.

Flourished the trumpets : entered Heart,
  A youth in crimson and gold.
Flourished again : Brain stood apart,
  Steel-armored, dark and cold.

III.

Heart's palfrey caracoled gayly round,
  Heart tra-li-ra'd merrily ;
But Brain sat still, with never a sound,
  So cynical-calm was he.

IV.

Heart's helmet-crest bore favors three
  From his lady's white hand caught ;
While Brain wore a plumeless casque ; not he
  Or favor gave or sought.

V.

The herald blew ; Heart shot a glance
　　To find his lady's eye,
But Brain gazed straight ahead his lance
　　To aim more faithfully.

VI.

They charged, they struck ; both fell, both bled.
　　Brain rose again, ungloved,
Heart, dying, smiled and faintly said,
　　" My love to my beloved ! "

CAMP FRENCH, WILMINGTON, N. C.,
　　　May, 1862.

JOUST SECOND.

I.

A-many sweet eyes wept and wept,
　　A-many bosoms heaved again ;
A-many dainty dead hopes slept
　　With yonder Heart-knight prone o' the plain.

II.

Yet stars will burn through any mists,
　　And the ladies' eyes, through rains of fate,
Still beamed upon the bloody lists
　　And lit the joust of Love and Hate.

III.

O strange ! or ere a trumpet blew,
　　Or ere a challenge-word was given,
A knight leapt down i' the lists ; none knew
　　Whether he sprang from earth or heaven.

IV.

His cheek was soft as a lily-bud,
   His grey eyes calmed his youth's alarm ;
Nor helm nor hauberk nor even a hood
   Had he to shield his life from harm.

V.

No falchion from his baldric swung,
   He wore a white rose in its place.
No dagger at his girdle hung,
   But only an olive-branch, for grace.

VI.

And " Come, thou poor mistaken knight,"
   Cried Love, unarmed, yet dauntless there,
' Come on, God pity thee !—I fight
   Sans sword, sans shield ; yet, Hate, beware ! "

VII.

Spurred furious Hate ; he foamed at mouth,
   His breath was hot upon the air,
His breath scorched souls, as a dry drought
   Withers green trees and burns them bare.

VIII.

Straight drives he at his enemy,
   His hairy hands grip lance in rest,
His lance it gleams full bitterly,
   God !---gleams, true-point, on Love's bare breast !

IX.

Love's grey eyes glow with a heaven-heat,
  Love lifts his hand in a saintly prayer ;
Look ! Hate hath fallen at his feet !
  Look ! Hate hath vanished in the air !

X.

Then all the throng looked kind on all ;
  Eyes yearned, lips kissed, dumb souls were freed ;
Two magic maids' hands lifted a pall
  And the dead knight, Heart, sprang on his steed.

XI.

Then Love cried, " Break me his lance, each knight !
  Ye shall fight for blood-athirst Fame no more ! "
And the knights all doffed their mailèd might
  And dealt out dole on dole to the poor.

XII.

Then dove-flights sanctified the plain,
  And hawk and sparrow shared a nest.
And the great sea opened and swallowed Pain,
  And out of this water-grave floated Rest !

MACON, GEORGIA, 1865.

THE DYING WORDS OF STONEWALL JACKSON.

"Order A. P. Hill to prepare for battle."
"Tell Major Hawks to advance the Commissary train."
"Let us cross the river and rest in the shade."

THE stars of Night contain the glittering Day
And rain his glory down with sweeter grace
Upon the dark World's grand, enchanted face—
    All loth to turn away.

And so the Day, about to yield his breath,
Utters the stars unto the listening Night,
To stand for burning fare-thee-wells of light
    Said on the verge of death.

O hero-life that lit us like the sun!
O hero-words that glittered like the stars
And stood and shone above the gloomy wars
    When the hero-life was done!

The phantoms of a battle came to dwell
I' the fitful vision of his dying eyes—
Yet even in battle-dreams, he sends supplies
    To those he loved so well.

His army stands in battle-line arrayed :
His couriers fly : all's done : now God decide !
—And not till then saw he the Other Side
    Or would accept the shade.

Thou Land whose sun is gone, thy stars remain !
Still shine the words that miniature his deeds.
O thrice-beloved, where'er thy great heart bleeds,
    Solace hast thou for pain !

GEORGIA, September, 1865.

TO WILHELMINA.

A WHITE face, drooping, on a bending neck :
  A tube-rose that with heavy petal curves
  Her stem : a foam-bell on a wave that swerves
Back from the undulating vessel's deck.

From out the whitest cloud of summer steals
  The wildest lightning : from this face of thine
  Thy soul, a fire-of-heaven, warm and fine,
In marvellous flashes its fair self reveals.

As when one gazes from the summer sea
  On some far gossamer cloud, with straining eye,
  Fearing to see it vanish in the sky,
So, floating, wandering Cloud-Soul, I watch thee.

MONTGOMERY, ALABAMA, 1866.

WEDDING-HYMN.

THOU God, whose high, eternal Love
   Is the only blue sky of our life,
Clear all the Heaven that bends above
   The life-road of this man and wife.

May these two lives be but one note
   In the world's strange-sounding harmony,
Whose sacred music e'er shall float
   Through every discord up to Thee.

As when from separate stars two beams
   Unite to form one tender ray:
As when two sweet but shadowy dreams
   Explain each other in the day :

So may these two dear hearts one light
   Emit, and each interpret each.
et an angel come and dwell to-night
   In this dear double-heart, and teach !

MACON, GEORGIA, September, 1865.

IN THE FOAM.

LIFE swelleth in a whitening wave,
And dasheth thee and me apart.
I sweep out seaward :—be thou brave.
    And reach the shore, Sweetheart.

Beat back the backward-thrusting sea.
Thy weak white arm his blows may thwart.
Christ buffet the wild surge for thee
    Till thou 'rt ashore, Sweetheart.

Ah, now thy face grows dim apace,
And seems of yon white foam a part.
Canst hear me through the water bass,
    Cry : " To the Shore, Sweetheart ? "

Now Christ thee soothe upon the Shore,
My lissome-armed sea-Britomart.
I sweep out seaward, never more
    To find the Shore, Sweetheart.

PRATTVILLE, ALABAMA, December, 1867.

BARNACLES.

MY soul is sailing through the sea,
But the Past is heavy and hindereth me.
The Past hath crusted cumbrous shells
That hold the flesh of cold sea-mells
    About my soul.
The huge waves wash, the high waves roll,
Each barnacle clingeth and worketh dole
    And hindereth me from sailing!

Old Past let go, and drop i' the sea
Till fathomless waters cover thee!
For I am living but thou art dead;
Thou drawest back, I strive ahead
    The Day to find.
Thy shells unbind! Night comes behind,
I needs must hurry with the wind
    And trim me best for sailing.

MACON, GEORGIA, 1867.

NIGHT.

FAIR is the wedded reign of Night and Day.
Each rules a half of earth with different sway,
Exchanging kingdoms, East and West, alway.

Like the round pearl that Egypt drunk in wine,
The sun half sinks i' the brimming, rosy brine :
The wild Night drinks all up : how her eyes shine !

Now the swift sail of straining life is furled,
And through the stillness of my soul is whirled
The throbbing of the hearts of half the world.

I hear the cries that follow Birth and Death.
I hear huge Pestilence draw his vaporous breath :
" Beware, prepare, or else ye die," he saith.

I hear a haggard student turn and sigh :
I hear men begging Heaven to let them die :
And, drowning all, a wild-eyed woman's cry.

So Night takes toll of Wisdom as of Sin.
The student's and the drunkard's cheek is thin :
But flesh is not the prize we strive to win.

Now airy swarms of fluttering dreams descend
On souls, like birds on trees, and have no end.
O God, from vulture-dreams my soul defend !

Let fall on Her a rose-leaf rain of dreams,
All passionate-sweet, as are the loving beams
Of starlight on the glimmering woods and streams.

MONTGOMERY, ALABAMA, April, 1866.

JUNE DREAMS, IN JANUARY.

" So pulse, and pulse, thou rhythmic-hearted Noon
    That liest, large-limbed, curved along the hills,
In languid palpitation, half a-swoon
    With ardors and sun-loves and subtle thrills ;

" Throb, Beautiful ! while the fervent hours exhale
    As kisses faint-blown from thy finger-tips
Up to the sun, that turn him passion-pale
    And then as red as any virgin's lips.

" O tender Darkness, when June-day hath ceased,
    —Faint Odor from the day-flower's crushing born,
—Dim, visible Sigh out of the mournful East
    That cannot see her lord again till morn :

" And many leaves, broad-palmèd towards the sky
    To catch the sacred raining of star-light :
And pallid petals, fain, all fain to die,
    Soul-stung by too keen passion of the night :

" And short-breath'd winds, under yon gracious moon
    Doing mild errands for mild violets,
Or carrying sighs from the red lips of June
    What aimless way the odor-current sets :

" And stars, ringed glittering in whorls and bells,
    Or bent along the sky in looped star-sprays,
Or vine-wound, with bright grapes in panicles,
    Or bramble-tangled in a sweetest maze,

" Or lying like young lilies in a lake
 About the great white Lotus of the moon,
Or blown and drifted, as if winds should shake
 Star blossoms down from silver stems too soon,

" Or budding thick about full open stars,
 Or clambering shyly up cloud-lattices,
Or trampled pale in the red path of Mars,
 Or trim-set in quaint gardener's fantasies :

" And long June night-sounds crooned among the leaves,
 And whispered confidence of dark and green,
And murmurs in old moss about old eaves,
 And tinklings floating over water-sheen ! "

Then he that wrote laid down his pen and sighed ;
And straightway came old Scorn and Bitterness,
Like Hunnish kings out of the barbarous land,
And camped upon the transient Italy
That he had dreamed to blossom in his soul.
" I 'll date this dream, he said ; so : 'Given, these,
On this, the coldest night in all the year,
From this, the meanest garret in the world,
In this, the greatest city in the land,
To you, the richest folk this side of death,
By one, the hungriest poet under heaven,
—Writ while his candle sputtered in the gust,
And while his last, last ember died of cold,
And while the mortal ice i' the air made free
Of all his bones and bit and shrunk his heart,
And while soft Luxury made show to strike
Her glovèd hands together and to smile
What time her weary feet unconsciously
Trode wheels that lifted Avarice to power,
—And while, moreover,—O thou God, thou God—

His worshipful sweet wife sat still, afar,
Within the village whence she sent him forth
Into the town to make his name and fame,
Waiting, all confident and proud and calm,
Till he should make for her his name and fame,
Waiting—O Christ, how keen this cuts !—large-eyed,
With Baby Charley till her husband make
For her and him a poet's name and fame.'
—Read me," he cried, and rose, and stamped his foot
Impatiently at Heaven, "read me this,"
(Putting th' inquiry full in the face of God)
" Why can we poets dream us beauty, so,
But cannot dream us bread ?   Why, now, can I
Make, aye, create this fervid throbbing June
Out of the chill, chill matter of my soul,
Yet cannot make a poorest penny-loaf
Out of this same chill matter, no, not one
For Mary though she starved upon my breast ? "
   And then he fell upon his couch, and sobbed,
And, late, just when his heart leaned o'er
The very edge of breaking, fain to fall,
God sent him sleep.
                There came his room-fellow,
Stout Dick, the painter, saw the written dream,
Read, scratched his curly pate, smiled, winked, fell on
The poem in big-hearted comic rage,
Quick folded, thrust in envelope, addressed
To him, the critic-god, that sitteth grim
And giant-grisly on the stone causeway
That leadeth to his magazine and fame.
   Him, by due mail, the little Dream of June
Encountered growling, and at unawares
Stole in upon his poem-battered soul
So that he smiled,—then shook his head upon 't
—Then growled, then smiled again, till at the last,

As one that deadly sinned against his will,
He writ upon the margin of the Dream
A wondrous, wondrous word that in a day
Did turn the fleeting song to very bread,
—Whereat Dick Painter leapt, the poet wept,
And Mary slept with happy drops a-gleam
Upon long lashes of her serene eyes
From twentieth reading of her poet's news
Quick-sent, " O sweet my Sweet, to dream is power,
And I can dream thee bread and dream thee wine,
And I will dream thee robes and gems, dear Love,
To clothe thy holy loveliness withal,
And I will dream thee here to live by me,
Thee and my little man thou hold'st at breast,
—Come, Name, come, Fame, and kiss my Sweetheart's feet ! "

GEORGIA, 1869.

NOTES.

NOTES.

SUNRISE, p. 3.

Sunrise, Mr. Lanier's latest completed poem, was written while his sun of life seemed fairly at the setting, and the hand which first penciled its lines had not strength to carry nourishment to the lips.

The three *Hymns of the Marshes* which open this collection are the only written portions of a series of six *Marsh Hymns* that were designed by the author to form a separate volume.

The *Song* of the Marshes, *At Sunset*, does not belong to this group, but is inserted among the *Hymns* as forming a true accord with them.

THE MARSHES OF GLYNN, p. 14.

The salt marshes of Glynn County, Georgia, immediately around the sea-coast city of Brunswick.

CLOVER, p. 19.

Clover is placed as the initial poem of a volume which was left in orderly arrangement among the author's papers. His own grouping in that volume has been followed as far as possible in this fuller collection.

THE MOCKING-BIRD, p. 27.

" . . . yon trim Shakespeare on the tree "

leads back, almost twenty years from its writing, to the poet's college note-book where we find the boy reflecting : " A poet is the mocking-bird of the spiritual universe. In him are collected all the individual songs of all individual natures."

CORN, p. 53.

Corn will hold a distinct interest for those who study the gathering forces in the author's growth : for it was the first outcome of his con-sciously-developing art-life. This life, the musician's and poet's, he entered upon—after years of patient denial and suppression—in September, 1873, uncertain of his powers but determined to give them wing.

His " fieldward-faring eyes took harvest " " among the stately corn-ranks," in a portion of middle Georgia sixty miles to the north of Macon. It is a high tract of country from which one looks across the lower reaches to the distant Blue Ridge mountains, whose wholesome breath, all unobstructed, here blends with the woods-odors of the beech, the hickory and the muscadine : a part of a range recalled elsewhere by Mr. Lanier, as " that ample stretch of generous soil, where the Appalachian ruggednesses calm themselves into pleasant hills before dying quite away into the sea-board levels "—where " a man can find such temperances of heaven and earth—enough of struggle with nature to draw out manhood, with enough of bounty to sanction the struggle —that a more exquisite co-adaptation of all blessed circumstances for man's life need not be sought."

MY SPRINGS, p. 71.

Of this newly-written poem Mr. Lanier says in a letter of March, 1874 : " Of course, since I have written it to print I cannot make it such as *I* desire in artistic design : for the forms of to-day require a certain trim smugness and clean-shaven propriety in the face and dress of a poem, and I must win a hearing by conforming in some degree to these tyrannies, with a view to overturning them in the future. Written so, it is not nearly so beautiful as I would have it ; and I therefore have another still in my heart, which I will some day write for myself."

A SONG OF LOVE, p. 97.

A Song of Love, like *Betrayal*, belongs to the early plan of *The Jacquerie*. It was written for one of the Fool's songs and, after several recastings, took its present shape in 1879.

TO NANNETTE FALK-AUERBACH, p. 102.

This sonnet was originally written in the German and published in a German daily of Baltimore, while the author's translation appeared at the same time in the Baltimore GAZETTE.

TO OUR MOCKING-BIRD, p. 103.

The history of this bird's life is given at length under the title of " Bob," in THE INDEPENDENT of August 3, 1882, and will show that he deserved to be immortal—as we hope he is.

ODE TO THE JOHNS HOPKINS UNIVERSITY, p. 108.

" . . . the soaring genius'd Sylvester
That earlier loosed the knot great Newton tied,"

An algebraic theorem announced by Newton was demonstrated and extended by Sylvester.—SIDNEY LANIER.

A Ballad of Trees and the Master, p. 141.

A Ballad of Trees and the Master was conceived as an interlude of the latest *Hymn of the Marshes, Sunrise*, although written earlier. In the author's first copy and first revision of that *Hymn*, the *Ballad* was incorporated, following the invocation to the trees which closes with :

> " And there, oh there
> As ye hang with your myriad palms upturned in the air,
> Pray me a myriad prayer."

In Mr. Lanier's final copy the *Ballad* is omitted. It was one of several interludes which he at first designed, but, for some reason, afterwards abandoned.

To My Class, p. 146.

A class in English Literature, composed of young girls who had been studying with Mr. Lanier *The Knighte's Tale* of Chaucer.

The sonnet *On Violet's Wafers* was addressed to a member of the same class, and is similarly conceived.

Under the Cedarcroft Chestnut, p. 149.

" This chestnut-tree (at Cedarcroft, the estate of Mr. Bayard Taylor, in Pennsylvania), is estimated to be more than eight hundred years old."—SIDNEY LANIER, 1877.

Hard by stood its mate, apparently somewhat younger. It is related in a letter of 1882, from Mrs. Taylor, that in 1880, a year after Mr. Taylor's death, one of these majestic trees gave the first signs of decay : while his comrade lingered two years longer—to follow as closely the footsteps of Mr. Lanier : the two, faithful-hearted " to their master and to him who sang of them."

A Florida Ghost, p. 171.

The incidents recorded of this storm are matter of history in and around Tampa.

Nine from Eight, p. 177.

The local expression " under the hack " is kindly explained by an authority in middle Georgia dialect, Richard Malcolm Johnston, author of *The Dukesborough Tales* and other Georgia stories. He says :

" ' Under the hack ' is a well-known phrase among the country-people, and is applied, generally in a humorous sense, to those who have been cowed by any accident. A man who is overruled by his wife, I have often heard described as ' under the hack ': ' She's got him under the hack.' So, when a man has lost spirit from any cause, he is said to be ' under the hack.' The phrase is possibly derived from ' hackle,' an instrument used in the breaking of flax."

" THAR'S MORE IN THE MAN," ETC., p. 180.

" Jones " designates Jones County, Ga., one of the counties adjoin-
ing Bibb County, in which Macon is located.

THE JACQUERIE, p. 191.

Although *The Jacquerie* remained a fragment for thirteen years Mr.
Lanier's interest in the subject never abated. Far on in this interval
he is found planning for leisure to work out in romance the story of
that savage insurrection of the French peasantry, which the Chronicles
of Froissart had impressed upon his boyish imagination.

To ——, p. 230.

The era of verse-writing with Mr. Lanier reopens in this dream of
the Virginia bay where poet's reveries and war's awakenings continu-
ally alternated.

He presents it for a friend's criticism—at the age of twenty-one—in
these words : " I send you a little poem which sang itself through me
the other day. 'Tis the first I've written in many years."

NIGHT, p. 240.

This poem was not published by the writer and the simile of the
second verse was appropriated to *An Evening Song*. This partial rep-
etition—like that of portions of *The Tournament* and of *A Dream of
June*, which occur in the *Psalm of the West*—will be pardoned as af-
fording a favorable opportunity to observe Mr. Lanier's growth in
artistic form.

THE CENTENNIAL CANTATA.

THE CENTENNIAL MEDITATION OF COLUMBIA.

1776–1876.

A CANTATA.

FROM this hundred-terraced height,
Sight more large with nobler light
Ranges down yon towering years.
Humbler smiles and lordlier tears
  Shine and fall, shine and fall,
While old voices rise and call
Yonder where the to-and-fro
Weltering of my Long-Ago
Moves about the moveless base
Far below my resting-place.

*MUSICAL AN-
NOTATIONS.*
*Full chorus:
sober, meas-
ured and yet
majestic
progressions
of chords.*

Mayflower, Mayflower, slowly hither flying,
Trembling westward o'er yon balking sea,
Hearts within *Farewell dear England* sighing,
Winds without *But dear in vain* replying,
Gray-lipp'd waves about thee shouted, crying
     "No!   It shall not be!"

*Chorus:
the sea and
the winds
mingling
their voices
with human
sighs.*

Jamestown, out of thee—
Plymouth, thee—thee, Albany—
Winter cries, *Ye freeze : away!*
Fever cries, *Ye burn :* away!
Hunger cries, *Ye starve :* away!
Vengeance cries, *Your graves shall stay!*

*Quartette:
a meagre
and despair-
ing minor.*

Then old Shapes and Masks of Things,

Fullchorus:
return of
the motive of
the second
movement,
but worked
up with
greater
fury, to the
climax of
the shout at
the last line.

Framed like Faiths or clothed like Kings
Ghosts of Goods once fleshed and fair,
Grown foul Bads in alien air—
War, and his most noisy lords,
Tongued with lithe and poisoned swords—
Error, Terror, Rage and Crime,
All in a windy night of time
Cried to me from land and sea,
                    No ! Thou shalt not be !

                    Hark !

Huguenots whispering *yea* in the dark,

A rapid
and intense
whisper-
chorus.

Puritans answering *yea* in the dark !
Yea like an arrow shot true to his mark,
Darts through the tyrannous heart of Denial.
Patience and Labor and solemn-souled Trial,
                    Foiled, still beginning,
                    Soiled, but not sinning,
Toil through the stertorous death of the Night,
Toil when wild brother-wars new-dark the Light,
Toil, and forgive, and kiss o'er, and replight.

Chorus of
jubilation,
until the ap-
peal of the
last two
lines intro-
duces a tone
of doubt : it
then sinks to
pianissimo.

Now Praise to God's oft-granted grace,
Now Praise to Man's undaunted face,
Despite the land, despite the sea,
I was : I am : and I shall be—
How long, Good Angel, O how long ?
Sing me from Heaven a man's own song !

Basso solo :
the good An-
gel replies :

" Long as thine Art shall love true love,
Long as thy Science truth shall know,
Long as thine Eagle harms no Dove,
Long as thy Law by law shall grow,

Long as thy God is God above,
Thy brother every man below,
So long, dear Land of all my love,
Thy name shall shine, thy fame shall glow ! "

O Music, fróm this height of time my Word un- *Full chorus:*
fold : *jubilation*
and
In tiiy large signals all men's hearts Man's heart *welcome.*
behold :
Mid-heaven unroll thy chords as friendly flags
unfurled,
And wave the world's best lover's welcome to the
world.

NOTE TO THE CANTATA.

The annotated musical directions which here accompany *The Can-
tata*, arranged for the composer's use, were first sent with the newly-
completed text in a private letter to Mr. Gibson Peacock, of Phila-
delphia.

I am enabled to give these annotations and the author's own introduc-
tion to his work through the kindness of Mr. Peacock : the friend who,
while yet an entire stranger, awakened and led the public recognition
of Mr. Lanier's place in the world of art.　　　M. D. L.

" BALTIMORE, January 18, 1876.

"　.　.　. The enclosed will show you partly what I have been
doing.　.　.　. The Centennial Commission has invited me to write
a poem which shall serve as the text for a Cantata (the music to be by
Dudley Buck, of New York), to be sung at the opening of the Exhibi-
tion, under Thomas' direction.　.　.　. I've written the enclosed.
Necessarily I had to think out the musical conceptions as well as the
poem, and I have briefly indicated these along the margin of each
movement.　I have tried to make the whole as simple and as candid as
a melody of Beethoven's : at the same time expressing the largest

ideas possible, and expressing them in such a way as could not be of-
fensive to any modern soul. I particularly hope you'll like the Angel's
song, where I have endeavored to convey, in one line each, the phi-
losophies of Art, of Science, of Power, of Government, of Faith, and of
Social Life. Of course I shall not expect that this will instantly appeal
to tastes peppered and salted by [certain of our contemporary writers] ;
but one cannot forget Beethoven, and somehow all my inspiration
came in these large and artless forms, in simple Saxon words, in un-
pretentious and purely intellectual conceptions, while nevertheless I
felt, all through, the necessity of making a genuine song—and not a
rhymed set of good adages—out of it. I adopted the trochees of the
first movement because they *compel* a measured, sober, and meditative
movement of the mind; and because, too, they are not the genius of
our language. When the troubles cease, and the land emerges as a
distinct unity, then I fall into our native iambics. . . ."

"BALTIMORE, January 25, 1876.

"MY DEAR FRIEND :—Your praise, and your wife's, give me a world
of comfort. I really do not believe anything was ever written under
an equal number of limitations ; and when I first came to know all the
conditions of the poem I was for a moment inclined to think that no
genuine work could be produced under them.

"As for the friend who was the cause of the compliment, it was, di-
rectly, Mr. Taylor. . . . *Indirectly*, *you* are largely concerned in
it. . . . I fancy [all] this must have been owing much to the repu-
tation which you set a-rolling so recently. . . .

"So, God bless you both.
"Your friend,　　　　　　　S. L."

AFTERWORD.

AFTERWORD.

A POET who is also a skilled professional musician would appear to have all sorts of advantages. Not only would he or she reunite the sundered halves of the power of control over melody and text which the Greeks called *mousikê*, thus reconstructing as well the type of Orpheus *in propria persona*. Having intimate knowledge of literal musical structure—its schemata of repetition, variation, and the modulation of relationships; its metaphors of gesture, event, and emotion —might seem to give one added insights into the so-called music of poetic language. Instances are of course rare: in the Renaissance, there is the case of Thomas Campion (yet even he was not a "professional" in the modern sense), and we are told of Herbert and Milton and their knowledge and love of music, their being able to play the lute, and so forth (but this is rather like being able to play the piano today: it doesn't make one a musician). Of nineteenth-century English poets, only Leigh Hunt and Robert Browning display much technical musical knowledge at all; in America, Whitman's exuberant love of opera is somewhat exceptional, and in general the English language has not tended to produce, in its writers of genius, the relations between literary and musical skills that we find in a Rousseau, an E. T. A. Hoffman, or a Nietzsche.

Sidney Lanier was extremely conscious of a dual heritage: a literal musical ancestry (Nicholas Lanier composed music for some of Ben Jonson's masques) and the figurative, but sometimes even more powerfully significant, literary paternity which is so fascinating in its manifest and latent variations. A professional orchestral flute-player of presumably great skill, Lanier was devoted to music and that devotion generally overflowed into his concern to sanctify poetry itself. But there is a danger for poetry always lurking in the literal, and this danger looms large in the literal conflation of poetry and music—save for that continuingly remarkable and tentative series of brief assignations which the long-since divorced couple, text and music, contrive for themselves from time to time in art-song. It can manifest itself in the proto-symbolist attempt to dissolve signification in what is thought to be "pure" sound, as in Poe: this is in itself a weakly literal misreading of the notion that Walter Pater would eventually put in canonical form as "All art constantly aspires toward the condition of music." Fortunately for Lanier's best poems, they are able to escape the reductive literalism that affected his prosodic and rhythmic theorizing and, as we shall see, the tropes of music in his poetry have much more to do with those of the major romantic tradition than with their author's own musicianship.

But even to consider the theory for a moment is instructive. Lanier's *The Science of English Verse*, finished in the penultimate year of the poet's life, when the final stages of tuberculosis were yet insufficiently debilitating to daunt his prodigious energies, is a touching monument to the mistake that organized linguistic sound patterns can be analyzed with the methods developed over centuries to notate musical tones. "Music is *not* a species of Language. Language is a species of music," Lanier insisted (Appendix VII in the Centennial Edition volume containing *The Science of English Verse*). In this he seemed unaware that some German romantic theorists before him, and much of the serious treatment of meaning and representation in music today, would either want to put it exactly the opposite way or argue that the very terms of the formulation are misleading. Lanier's concept of musicality in poetry, while it takes on an almost religious significance for him in itself, is derived from the sophisticated practical knowledge of a working musician; nevertheless, it is that very technical power which seems to turn the gentlest of spirits into an unwitting intellectual Procrustes.

Lanier's equivocal musical notations of prosodic entities—transcribing lines and passages of English accentual-syllabic verse in regularly-barred rhythmic notation—dictated a reading of the text rather than describing the activity of rhythmic linguistic events occurring in a metrical frame. He seemed unaware—as most nineteenth-century musicians were—of unbarred medieval and renaissance notation, or of the utility of *ad hoc* rebarrings as in later music. The notational possibilities open to him were thus rather narrow in the first place, causing him to interpret in triple or quadruple musical meters what are in fact subtle variations of what is only metaphorically speaking "length" or "duration" in accentual-syllabic verse. In essence, Lanier's musical notations were unpitched musical settings of the text, declamatory and inexpressive, seemingly responsible only to regularities of poetic accent better rendered by the standard notation of stressed and unstressed syllables in any case. None of his paradigms could be right or wrong, save for doing unreasonable violence to English word accent. Thus, for example, he notates the Old English "Wanderer," beginning "Oft him anhaga are gebideth," in musical 3/8 time; yet doing so in 2/4 would preserve similarly the downbeats on the primary stresses ("*oft*," "*an*," "*ar-*," and "*bid-*"), and even allow the secondary stress on the fourth syllable of the line a more viable rhythmic treatment than a triple rhythm does (unless Lanier were to have specified something like a muzurka rhythm for his second measure). But the point is ultimately that equal timing of syllables is in the case of English an irrelevant imposition of a declamatory chant upon the far more subtle, variable, and dynamic rhythms of the spoken language, and, even more important, that with a stressed language like English, the interplay of syntax and rhythm, the subtle dispositions of metrically stressed syllables to differentiate meanings (rather than, as Lanier felt, to set up an authenticating undersong of transcendence) is the heart of the rhythmic matter.

In such questions as that of rhyme too, odd, vague analogies between vowel sound, musical timbre, and visual "color," curiosities of some late eighteenth-century aesthetic theories, again come up in despite of deeper questions of signification. Lanier is concerned with feeling and not with meaning, both in music and in poetic language. His remarks on Beethoven's Seventh Symphony in one of his essays concern not the structure of the work but a program of emotionally mimetic moments and devices which he reads into it. In short, his technical writing on the music of verse generally expands upon a typical late-romantic trope, and as such might be considered part of his poetry.

His own verse on formal musical subjects reflects not so much his musical ability per se as it does his rather broadly held association of music with the divine. The poems to Beethoven and Wagner praise the composers as mythmakers and heroes of the imagination, and a sonnet to a Baltimore pianist both in German and in English invokes the conceptual hyperbole that, in her, Beethoven "lives again." Robert Browning, an amateur musician but a very hard-thinking one, might have been far more specific, as well as far more conditional, in a case like this, making very specific emblems and conceits out of sudden modulations, the architectonic character of certain kinds of musical structure (Beethoven's in particular, although for Lanier it is just that quality which ceases to exist in his sweeping but undifferentiated praise). It is indeed rare to find such precise musical imagery in Lanier's poems, as in the Browningesque

moment from the fine, late "Sunrise" when a line of almost
pure Whitman is followed with a varied repetition: "So,
with your question embroid'ring the dark of the question
of man, — / So, with your silences purfling this silence of
man." Here, "purfling," used so as to seem simply synony-
mous with "embroid'ring," is actually operating in its musi-
cal application—the purfling of black around the borders of
violins, violas, and cellos—to reinforce the relation of
"dark" to "silence." Similarly, the moment in "The Sym-
phony" when "A velvet flute-note fell down pleasantly /
Upon the bosom of that harmony," a precisely-observed
effect of orchestration, of flute against thick string-writing,
is being remembered. The interplay of flute and violin, fre-
quent in this and other poems, reverses a very traditional
sort of emblematic distinction (between the rational string
and the emotive wind), neoclassical in origin and ubiquitous
since the Renaissance, in another, far more personal musical
iconography. The violin of passion, whose sounds are pro-
duced by active bowing, is opposed frequently in his images
to the more controlled and rational flute. Again, from
"Sunrise":

> Oh, what if a sound should be made!
> Oh, what if a bound should be laid
> To this bow-and-string tension of beauty and silence a-spring,—
> To the bend of beauty the bow, or the hold of silence the string!
> I fear me . . .

Aside from the remarkable complexity of the image of
bow and string and the sense of their dialectic, these lines
suggest some of what G. M. Hopkins was writing at the
same time, but which would remain unpublished for so long.

Indeed, many of Lanier's remarkable lines have a power
that seems to be sapped by the overall structure of the
poems that contain them—and this is particularly true of
the chant-like Hymns. Three lines near the opening of
"Sunrise" need only to be deprived of the rhyme at the end
of the middle one to gain a Whitmanian strength:

> The little green leaves would not let me alone in my sleep;
> Up-breathed from the marshes, a message of range and of sweep,
> Interwoven with waftures of wild sea-liberties, drifting.

Or the opening line of "The Marshes of Glynn," when separated from the weaker, rhyming second one: "Glooms of the live-oaks, beautiful-braided and woven"; here again we feel that the music of Lanier's verse lies closer to the ebb and flow of Whitman's than to the brilliant contraptions of Swinburne's. These are both poets whose mighty conceptions of art, self, and sexuality could not but cause Lanier some concern, given his milder-natured belief in music as "Love in search of a word."

His most ambitious poems are the long, ode-like chants: "The Symphony," "Sunrise," "The Marshes of Glynn," "The Psalm of the West," the earlier "Corn." It is primarily moments in these that are most profoundly successful (with the exception, probably, of "Sunrise" and "The Marshes of Glynn," which are two of his finest poems). When he writes in a smaller compass, as is the very fine "A Ballad of Trees and the Master" or in "The Song of the Chattahoochee," he avoids the impulse to call attention to the expansive repetitions and modulating line-lengths of the more self-proclaimedly "musical" form, and this tends sometimes to undercut—as we have seen from a few examples—the particular rhetorical power of particular lines. It is instructive to compare the last-mentioned lyric, the voice of the poet-river dutifully shunning distractions of folly or dalliance (despite its "lover's pain to attain the plain," the Georgia river must shun the patently erotic "lures with the lights of streaming stone / In the clefts of the hills of Habersham, In the beds of the valleys of Hall"), with a later poet's revision of it. Hart Crane's "Repose of Rivers" recasts Lanier's stream as strongly as the earlier poet had recast Tennyson (both in "The Brook" and in other lyrics); "The pond I entered once and quickly fled— / I remember now its singing willow rim," is part of a meditative lyric, brood-

ing over a refigured journey whose distractions and byways
are as much its matter as is its mere termination.

This poem, along with the wonderful sonnet "To the
Mockingbird," "Clover," and the longer poems mentioned
earlier, comprise the canon of Lanier's poetry, and are of a
stature far above that of his occasional verses, or of his best-
forgotten verses in dialect. In them, he continually invokes
literal and figurative music as a trope for universal expres-
siveness. What is so interesting about this is how often he
employs or develops a figure from the history of English
poetry after Milton, such as the adaptation of the Aeolian
harp image into a natural instrument, in "The Psalm of
the West":

> And the sun stretched beams to the worlds as the shining strings
> Of the large hid harp that sounds when an all-lover sings.

Again, a few lines later in the same poem, the raising of
Pandemonium in Book II of *Paradise Lost* is echoed in the
musico-poetic artist's creation:

> And the spirals of music e'er higher and higher he wound
> Till the luminous cinctures of melody up from the ground
> Arose as the shaft of a tapering tower of sound . . .

It is more important for Lanier as a poet that this represents
the discerning ear of the reader of texts rather than that of
the performing reader of scores; Lanier's music is here
drawn from the repository of romantic musical mythology
rather than actual concert-hall practice, and it allows the
verse in which it is framed to become truly poetry rather
than versified essay or journalism.

It is by the very virtue of the way in which Lanier's work
in verse and prose embraces two modes of considering
music, then, that he holds such interest for readers inter-
ested in the relation of the two arts. If his prosodic theories
do not hold up, largely because of the weakness of their
theoretical grasp of linguistic structure, they certainly sup-
port in another, figurative way the larger thematic image,
the realm of the Sublime, that music becomes in his best

poems. Lanier's life as a practical musician could double with his vocation as a poet, and allowed him to sanctify artistic work—as against a rather simplistic vision of trade and industry—in more than one way. One cannot tell whether, had he lived beyond the age of thirty-nine, this vision might have acquired more complexity, or its expression more tension. But that the poems of 1880 (the year before his death) show him beginning to hit a remarkable stride, there can never be any doubt.

JOHN HOLLANDER